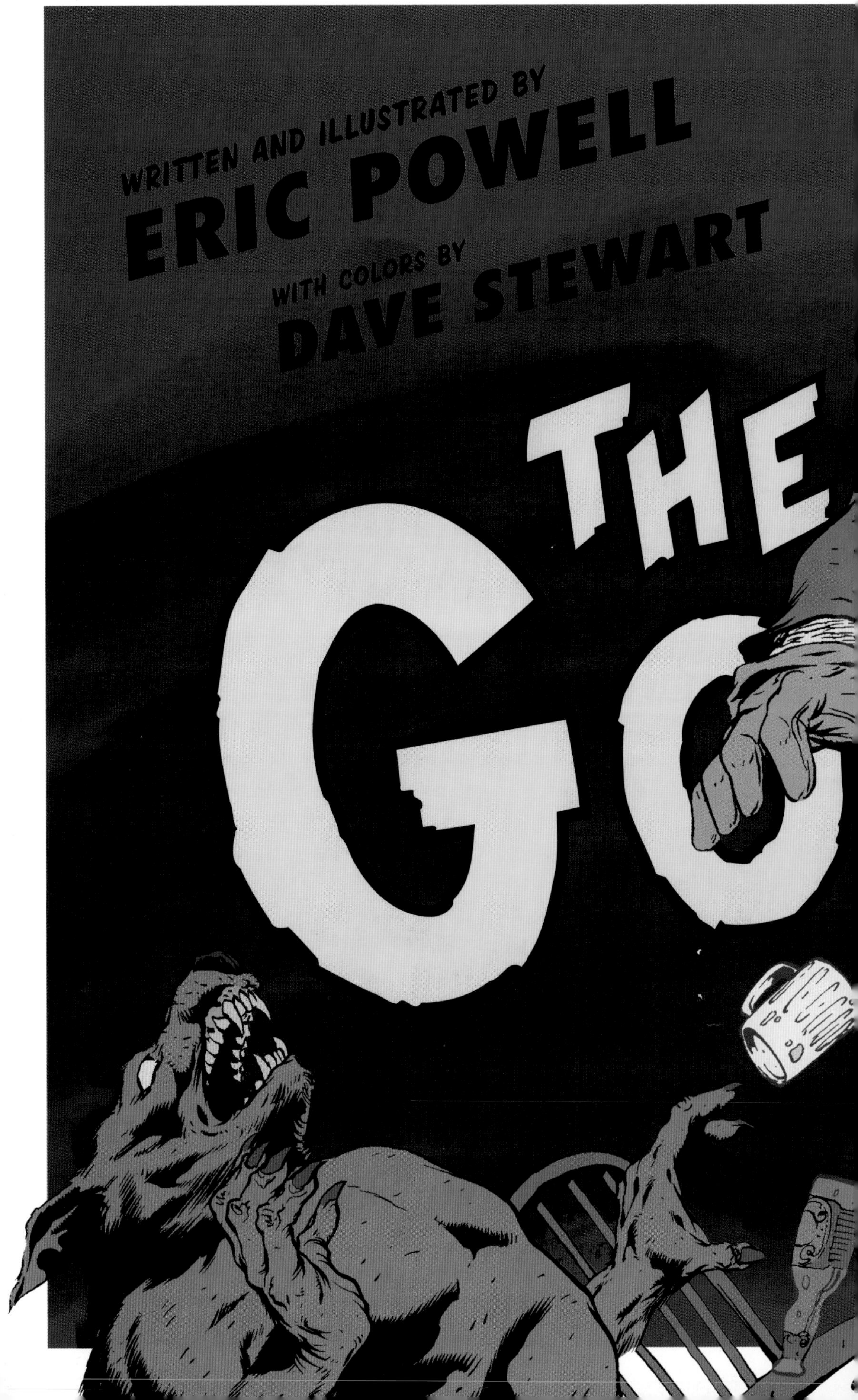
WRITTEN AND ILLUSTRATED BY
ERIC POWELL
WITH COLORS BY
DAVE STEWART
THE
GO

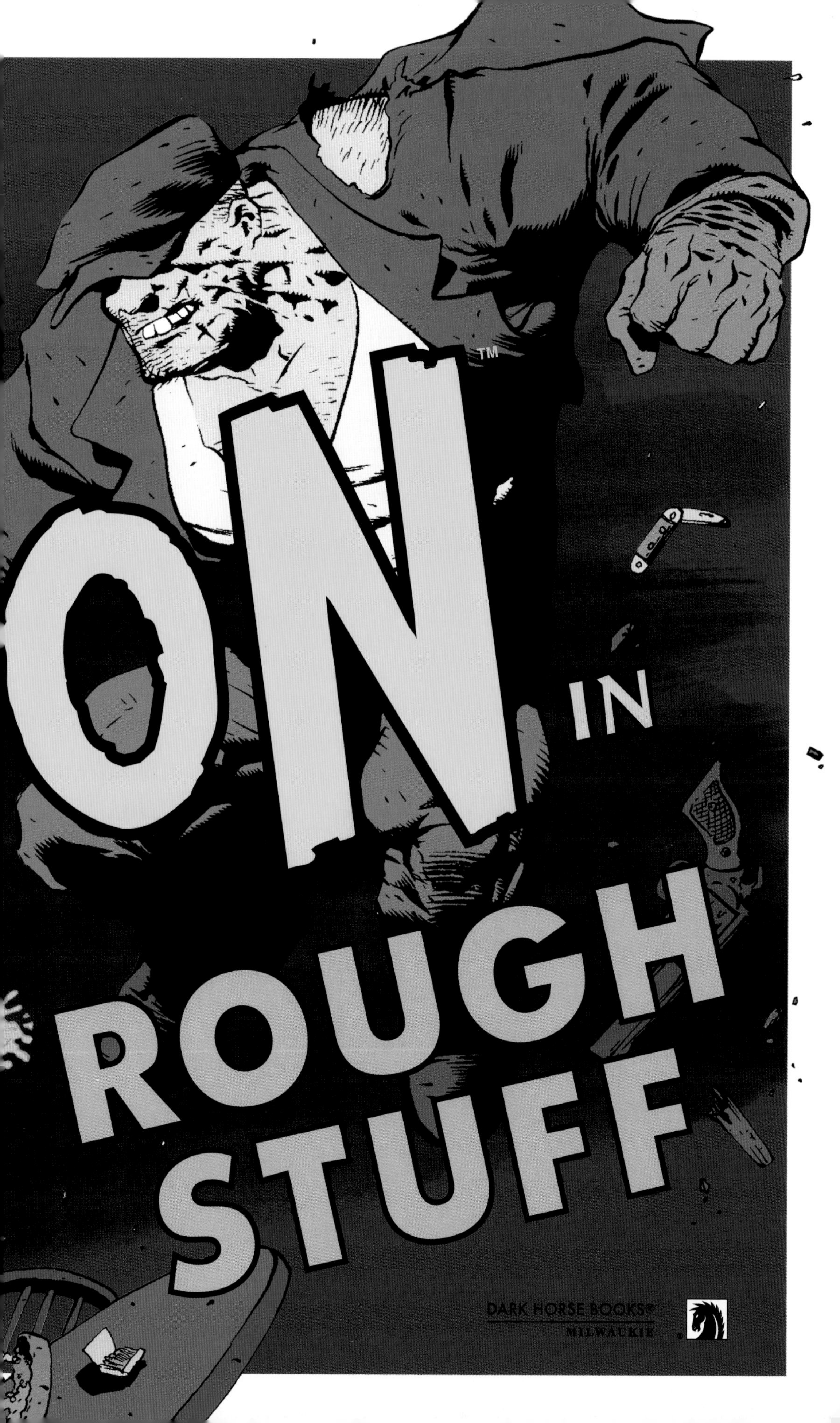
ON™
IN
ROUGH
STUFF

DARK HORSE BOOKS®
MILWAUKIE

*First Dark Horse edition:*

*editors* SCOTT ALLIE & MATT DRYER

*Second Dark Horse edition:*

*editor* SCOTT ALLIE

*associate editor* SIERRA HAHN

*assistant editor* FREDDYE LINS

*designer* AMY ARENDTS

*president & publisher* MIKE RICHARDSON

Neil Hankerson *executive vice president* • Tom Weddle *chief financial officer* • Randy Stradley *vice president of publishing* • Michael Martens *vice president of business development* • Anita Nelson *vice president of marketing, sales, and licensing* • David Scroggy *vice president of product development* • Dale LaFountain *vice president of information technology* • Darlene Vogel *director of purchasing* • Ken Lizzi *general counsel* • Davey Estrada *editorial director* • Scott Allie *senior managing editor* • Chris Warner *senior books editor* • Diana Schutz *executive editor* • Cary Grazzini *director of design and production* • Lia Ribacchi *art director* • Cara Niece *director of scheduling*

THE GOON™: ROUGH STUFF

This volume collects issues #1–#3 of *The Goon* Volume 1, originally published in 1999 and collected in *The Goon: Rough Stuff* from Albatross Exploding Funny Books.

Published by
Dark Horse Books
A division of
Dark Horse Comics, Inc.
10956 SE Main Street
Milwaukie, OR 97222

darkhorse.com

To find a comics shop in your area,
call the Comic Shop Locator Service toll-free at (888) 266-4226.

First Dark Horse edition: February 2004
Second Dark Horse edition: January 2010
ISBN 978-1-59582-468-4

10 9 8 7 6 5 4 3 2 1

Printed in China

# REGARDING THIS EDITION

Hello,

The only reason I'm allowing this book to be printed again is because I also like to see when artists I like sucked. I weather the embarrassment because I love you readers so much. That, and I gots bills to pay.

Sincerely,
Eric Powell
2009

# REGARDING THE 2004 DARK HORSE FIRST EDITION

Well, thanks for buying this crap again. If it's for the first time, my deepest apologies. First off, I'd like to thank the best colorist in the business, Dave Stewart, for working this project into his extremely busy schedule. Although I feel the quality of my drawings in this book are not up to snuff, it's still great to collaborate with someone of his ability.

When I was working on the first *Goon* in '98, it seemed pretty unrealistic to think anything would come of it. I drew it anyway. Due to unfortunate circumstances, the first run only lasted the three issues that are collected in this book. After the rights reverted back to me I decided to commit sure financial suicide and self-publish it. Fortunately it went well, Dark Horse picked it up, and 2003 was an unbelievably surreal break-out year.

What I'm getting at is that I just had to do this comic. If there is anything to divine cosmic destiny, which I doubt, then I'm destined to draw a funny book about a bucktoothed guy who punches zombies and hoboes. Hopefully that makes you feel a little better 'bout yourselves.

My deepest and sincerest thanks to all you *Goon* fans!

Eric Powell
Somewhere in the woods of middle Tennessee
2003

# *FOREWORD TO THE ALBATROSS EDITION*

This collection of my first three-issue series of *The Goon* is entitled *Rough Stuff* for a reason. If you're looking for the clean, refined work of an artist at the peak of his ability, or the steady, compelling storytelling of an established writer, you've come to the wrong place. Now, if you, like me, are a freak about wanting to see each step along the way of the process a creator takes in developing his skill, you may find this book entertaining. Before *The Goon* #1, I had not written a full-length comic, and my art, to say the least, was a bit crude. It looks like I inked some of this stuff with an electric toothbrush. You'll probably find some of this material pretty stupid. I'm inclined to agree. But it was never my intention to make an intellectual comic. In my humble opinion there are too many people trying (note that I said trying) to do that already. *The Goon* was always intended to be one thing . . . fun. Even in this rough stage, I believe it accomplishes that.

Oh, and by the way, if this is your first exposure to *The Goon*, pick up the new series. It makes this stuff look like crap.

Eric Powell
2002

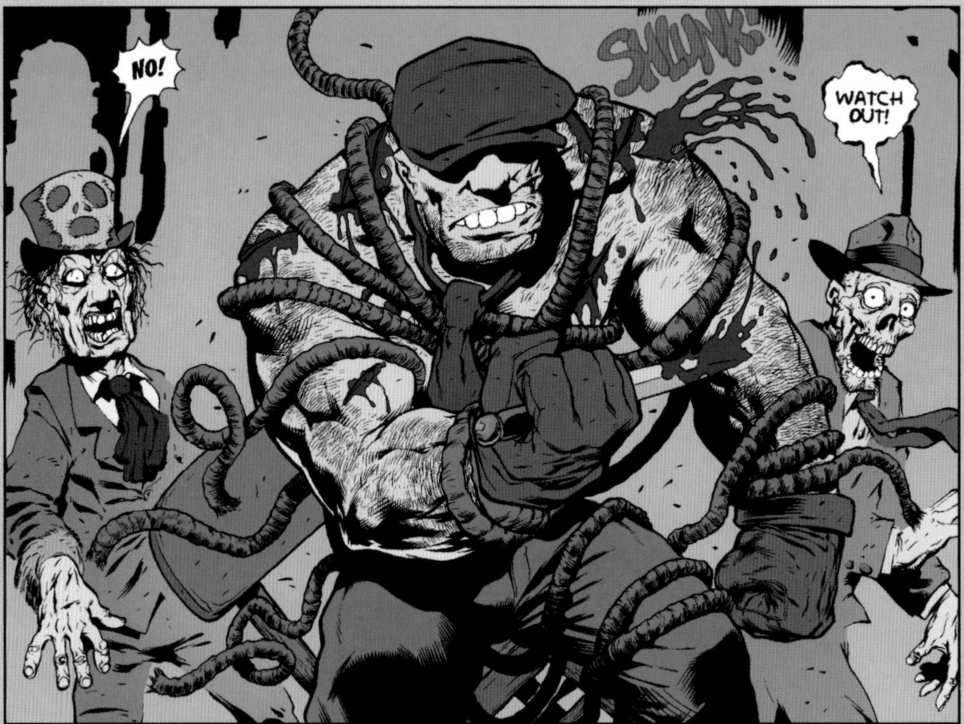
NO!
WATCH OUT!

# ROUGH STUFF: MILKING-IT-FOR-ALL-IT'S-WORTH EDITION, A SPECIAL INTRODUCTION BY MR. GOON AND MR. FRANKY

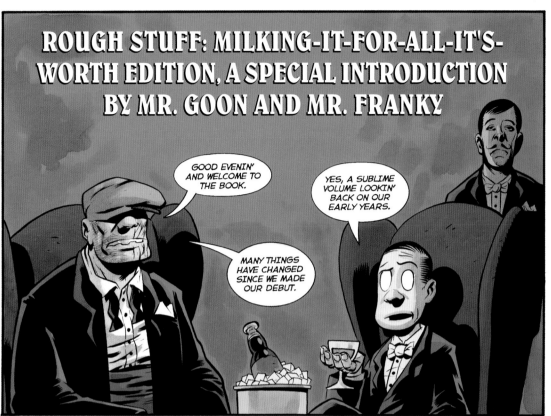

GOOD EVENIN' AND WELCOME TO THE BOOK.

YES, A SUBLIME VOLUME LOOKIN' BACK ON OUR EARLY YEARS.

MANY THINGS HAVE CHANGED SINCE WE MADE OUR DEBUT.

FOR ONE, I NO LONGER LOOK LIKE A SHAVED MULE.

AND I NO LONGER LOOK LIKE A BEADY EYED WEINER-HEAD.

THAT'S DEBATABLE.

QUIET, YOU!

BUT THE BIGGEST CHANGE HAS BEEN OUR FINANCIAL SITUATION.

YES, NOW THAT WE IS AT DARK HORSE, WE IS ALL HIGH CLASS AND DRINK ALL MANNERS OF WINES AND CHARDONNAYS, AS WELL.

AND YOU MAY NOTICE OUR NEW BOOKS IS A LITTLE DIFFERENT THAN WHAT'S IN THIS ONE.

YEAH, LIKE WE DON'T HAVE TALKIN' CHAINSAWS NO MORE.

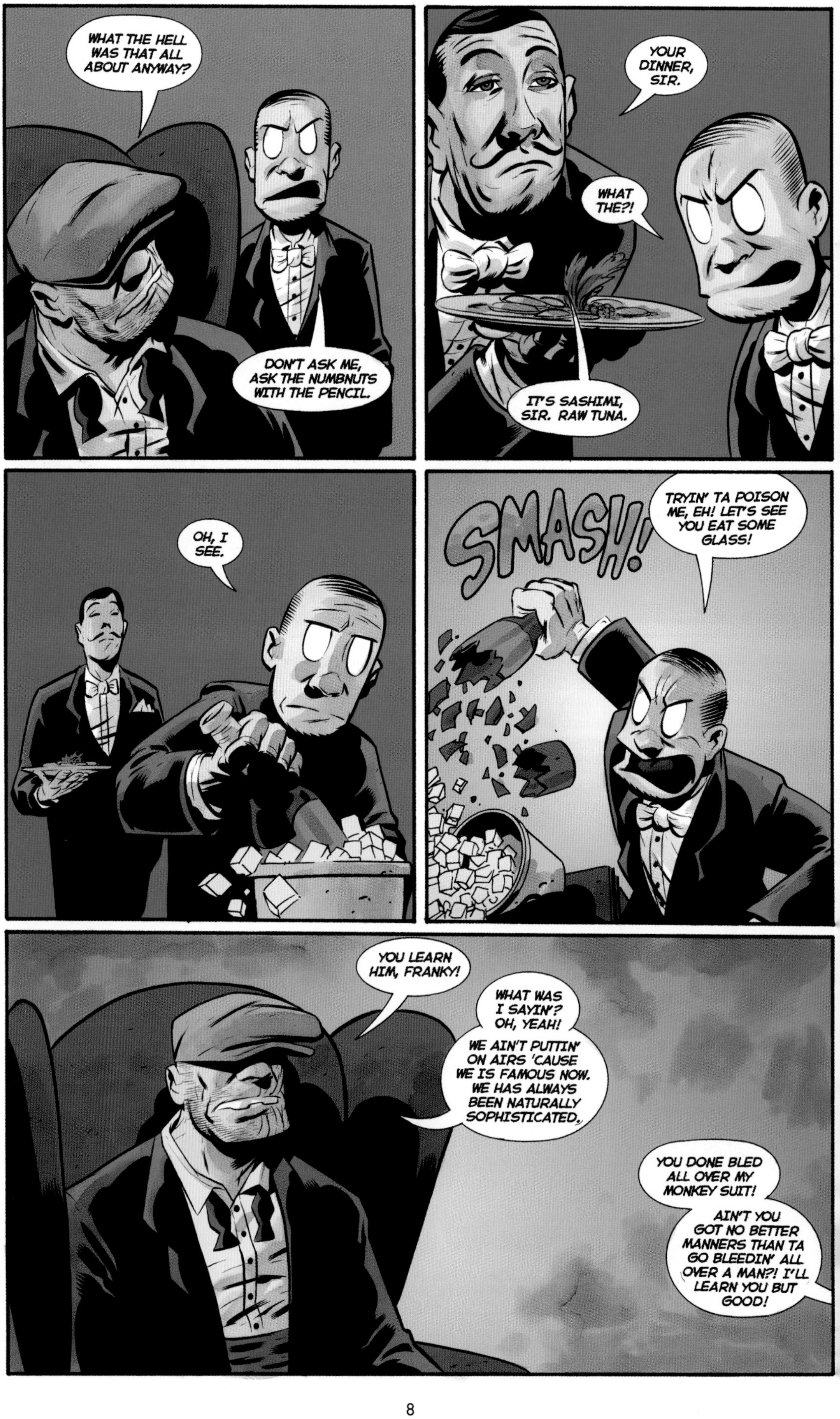
WHAT THE HELL WAS THAT ALL ABOUT ANYWAY?
DON'T ASK ME, ASK THE NUMBNUTS WITH THE PENCIL.
YOUR DINNER, SIR.
WHAT THE?!
IT'S SASHIMI, SIR. RAW TUNA.
OH, I SEE.
SMASH!
TRYIN' TA POISON ME, EH! LET'S SEE YOU EAT SOME GLASS!
YOU LEARN HIM, FRANKY!
WHAT WAS I SAYIN'? OH, YEAH!
WE AIN'T PUTTIN' ON AIRS 'CAUSE WE IS FAMOUS NOW. WE HAS ALWAYS BEEN NATURALLY SOPHISTICATED.
YOU DONE BLED ALL OVER MY MONKEY SUIT!
AIN'T YOU GOT NO BETTER MANNERS THAN TA GO BLEEDIN' ALL OVER A MAN?! I'LL LEARN YOU BUT GOOD!

# CHAPTER 1

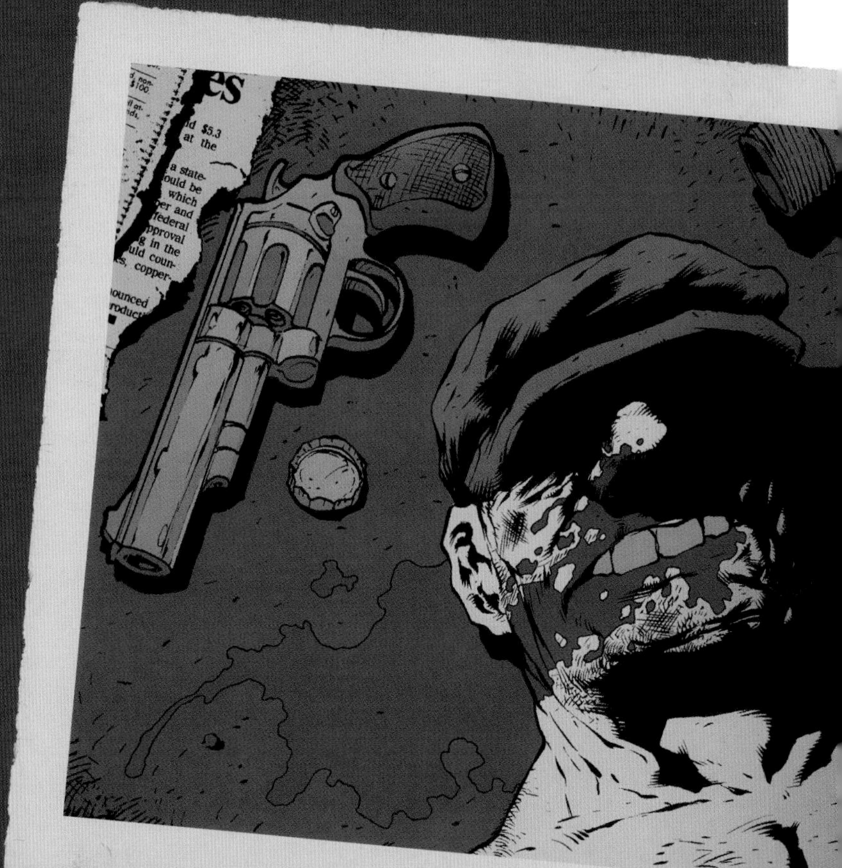

$5.3
at the
a state-
ould be
which
per and
federal
pproval
g in the
uld coun-
s, copper-
ounced
roduct

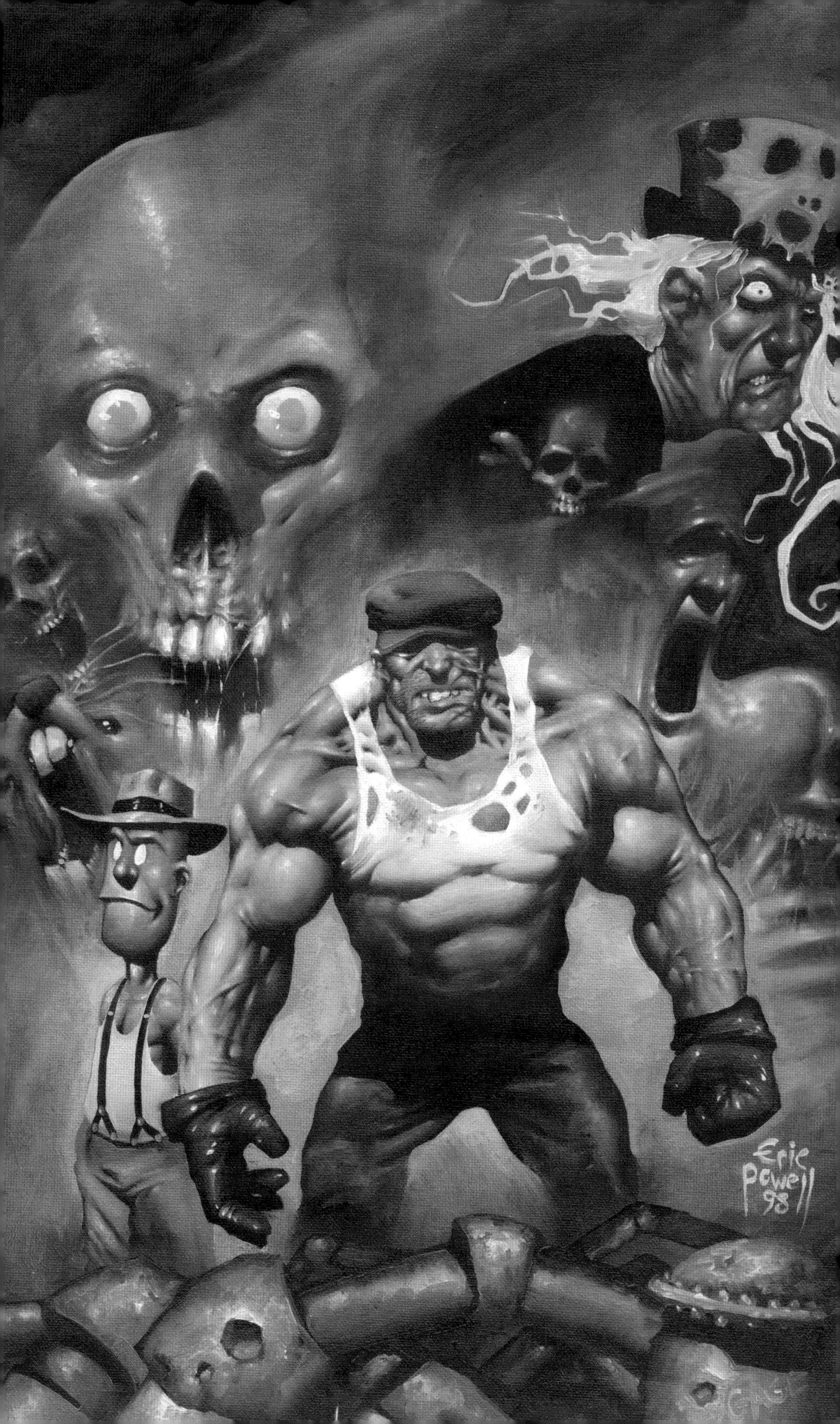
Eric Powell 98

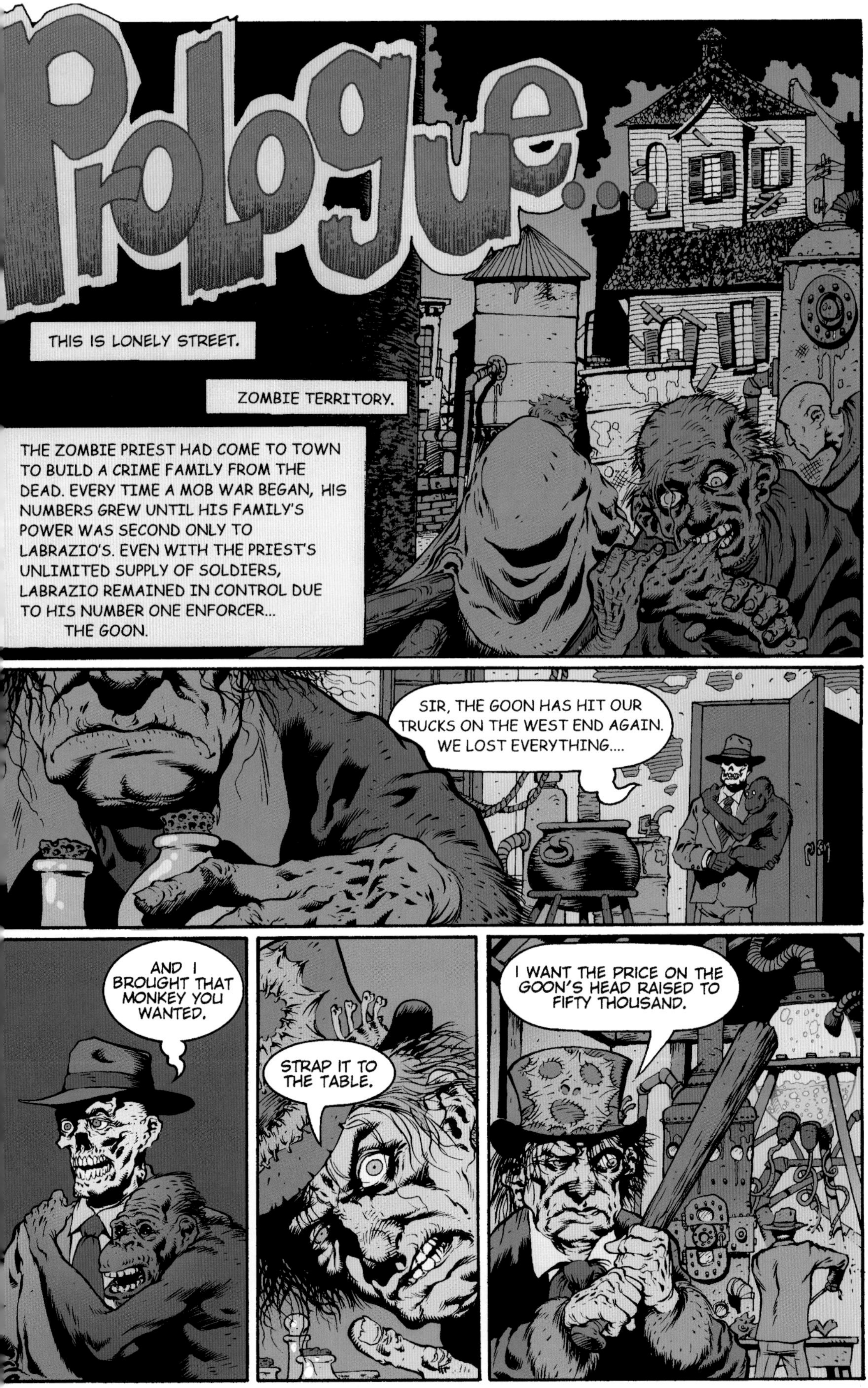
Prologue...
THIS IS LONELY STREET.
ZOMBIE TERRITORY.
THE ZOMBIE PRIEST HAD COME TO TOWN TO BUILD A CRIME FAMILY FROM THE DEAD. EVERY TIME A MOB WAR BEGAN, HIS NUMBERS GREW UNTIL HIS FAMILY'S POWER WAS SECOND ONLY TO LABRAZIO'S. EVEN WITH THE PRIEST'S UNLIMITED SUPPLY OF SOLDIERS, LABRAZIO REMAINED IN CONTROL DUE TO HIS NUMBER ONE ENFORCER... THE GOON.
SIR, THE GOON HAS HIT OUR TRUCKS ON THE WEST END AGAIN. WE LOST EVERYTHING....
AND I BROUGHT THAT MONKEY YOU WANTED.
STRAP IT TO THE TABLE.
I WANT THE PRICE ON THE GOON'S HEAD RAISED TO FIFTY THOUSAND.

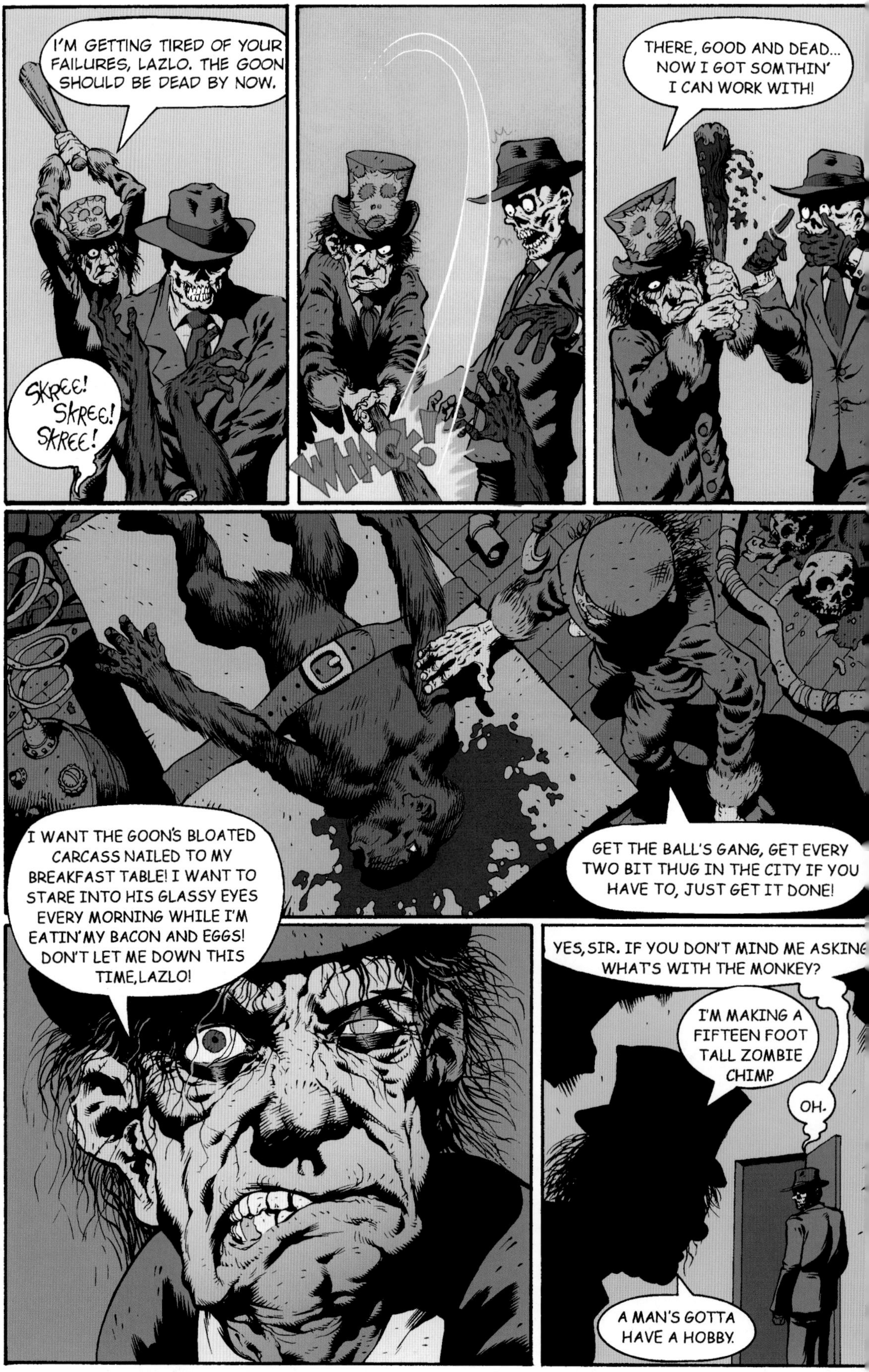
I'M GETTING TIRED OF YOUR FAILURES, LAZLO. THE GOON SHOULD BE DEAD BY NOW.
SKREE! SKREE! SKREE!
WHACK!
THERE, GOOD AND DEAD... NOW I GOT SOMTHIN' I CAN WORK WITH!
I WANT THE GOON'S BLOATED CARCASS NAILED TO MY BREAKFAST TABLE! I WANT TO STARE INTO HIS GLASSY EYES EVERY MORNING WHILE I'M EATIN' MY BACON AND EGGS! DON'T LET ME DOWN THIS TIME, LAZLO!
GET THE BALL'S GANG, GET EVERY TWO BIT THUG IN THE CITY IF YOU HAVE TO, JUST GET IT DONE!
YES, SIR. IF YOU DON'T MIND ME ASKING WHAT'S WITH THE MONKEY?
I'M MAKING A FIFTEEN FOOT TALL ZOMBIE CHIMP.
OH.
A MAN'S GOTTA HAVE A HOBBY.

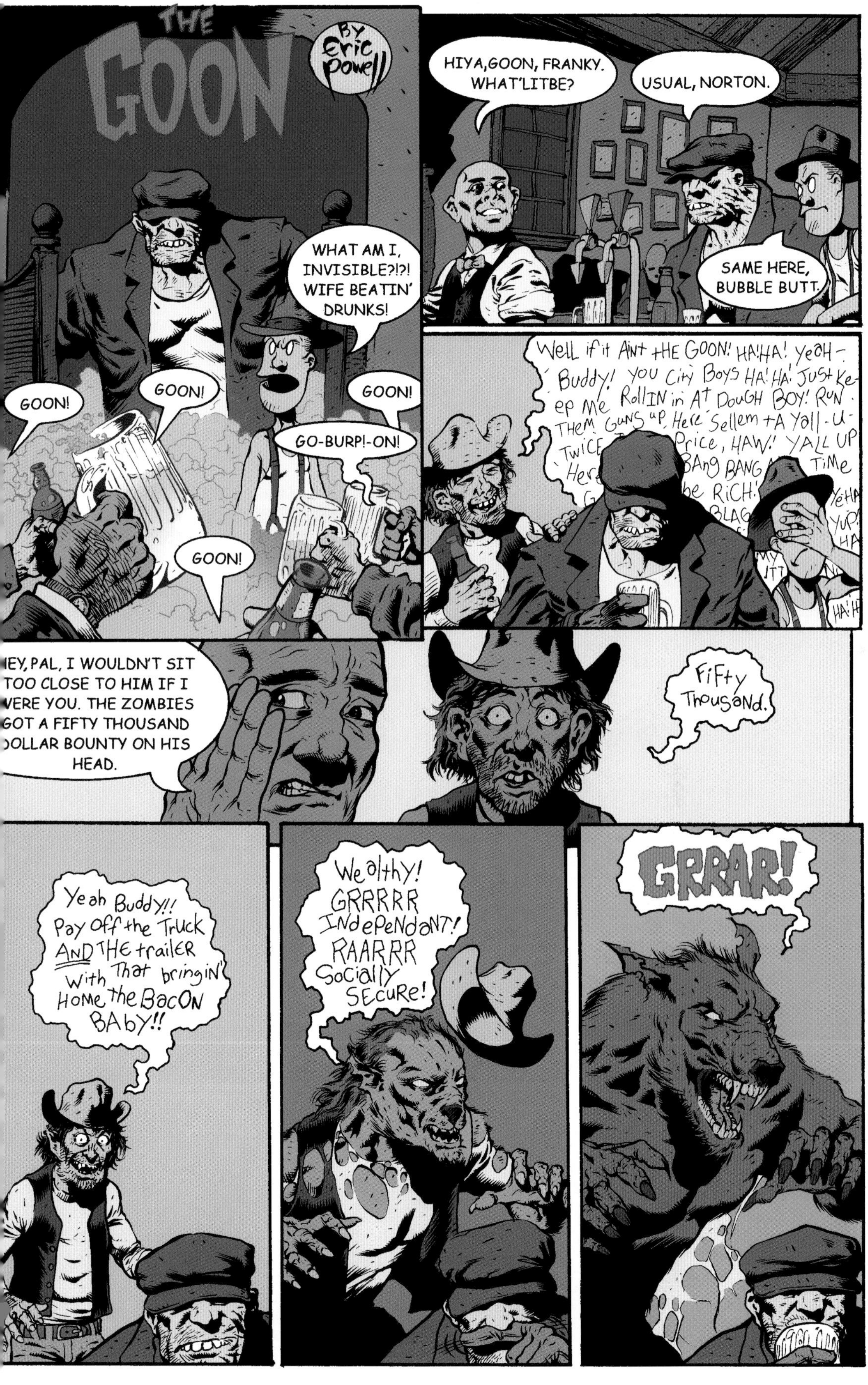
THE GOON
By Eric Powell
WHAT AM I, INVISIBLE?!?! WIFE BEATIN' DRUNKS!
GOON!
GOON!
GOON!
GO-BURP!-ON!
GOON!
HIYA, GOON, FRANKY. WHAT'LITBE?
USUAL, NORTON.
SAME HERE, BUBBLE BUTT.
Well if it AINT tHE GOON! HA!HA! yeaH- Buddy! you City Boys HA! HA! Just Keep Me RollIN in AT DouGH BOY! RUN THEM GUNS up Here Sellem tA Yall-U-TWICE Price, HAW! YALL UP BAng BANG TiMe be RiCH!
YeHA YUP! HA
HA! H
HEY, PAL, I WOULDN'T SIT TOO CLOSE TO HIM IF I WERE YOU. THE ZOMBIES GOT A FIFTY THOUSAND DOLLAR BOUNTY ON HIS HEAD.
Fifty Thousand.
Yeah Buddy!! Pay off the Truck AND THE trailer With That bringin' Home the BacON BAby!!
Wealthy! GRRRRR Independant! RAARRR Socially SEcuRe!
GRRAR!

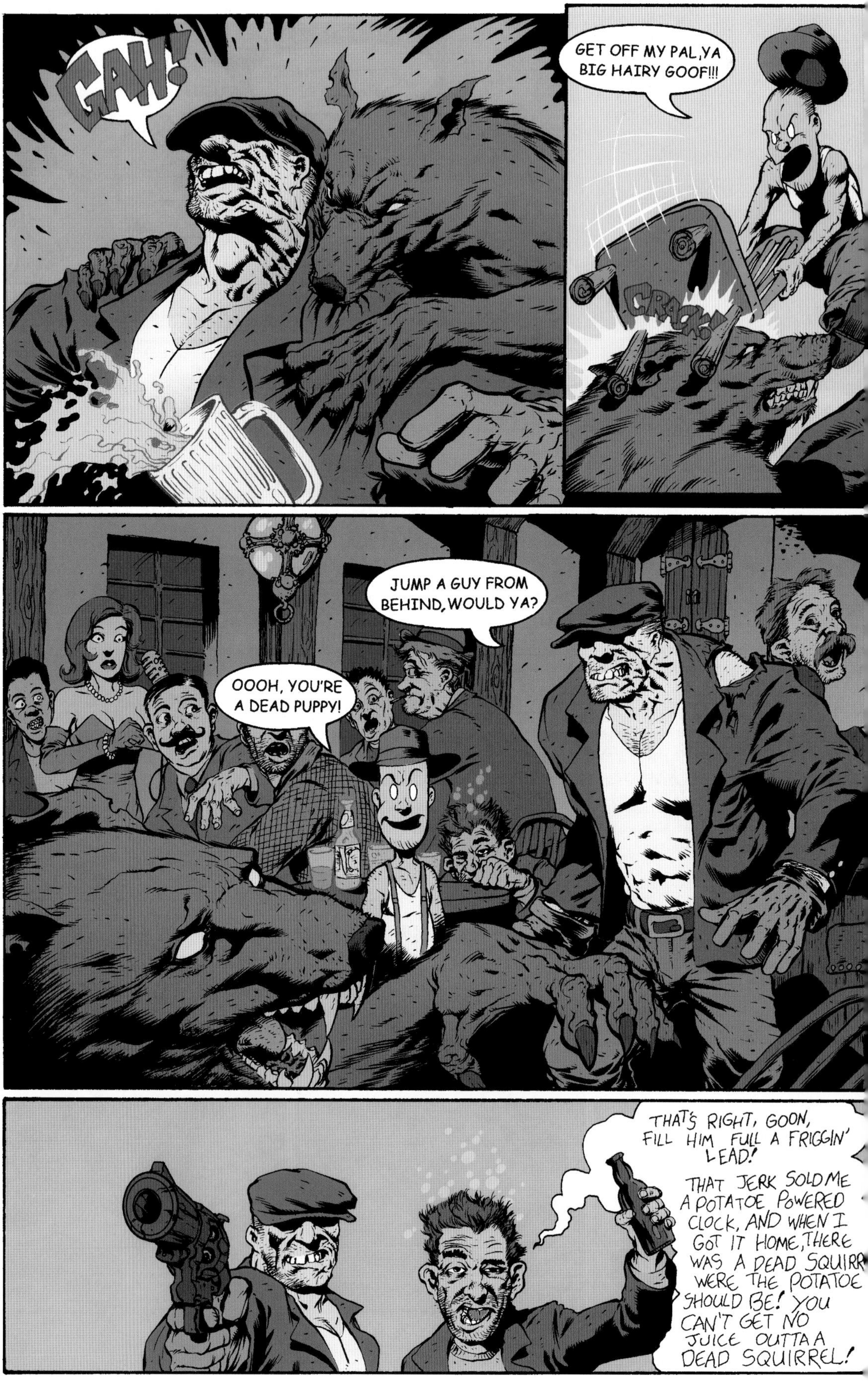
GAH!
GET OFF MY PAL, YA BIG HAIRY GOOF!!!
CRACK!
JUMP A GUY FROM BEHIND, WOULD YA?
OOOH, YOU'RE A DEAD PUPPY!
THAT'S RIGHT, GOON, FILL HIM FULL A FRIGGIN' LEAD!
THAT JERK SOLD ME A POTATOE POWERED CLOCK, AND WHEN I GOT IT HOME, THERE WAS A DEAD SQUIRR WERE THE POTATOE SHOULD BE! YOU CAN'T GET NO JUICE OUTTA A DEAD SQUIRREL!

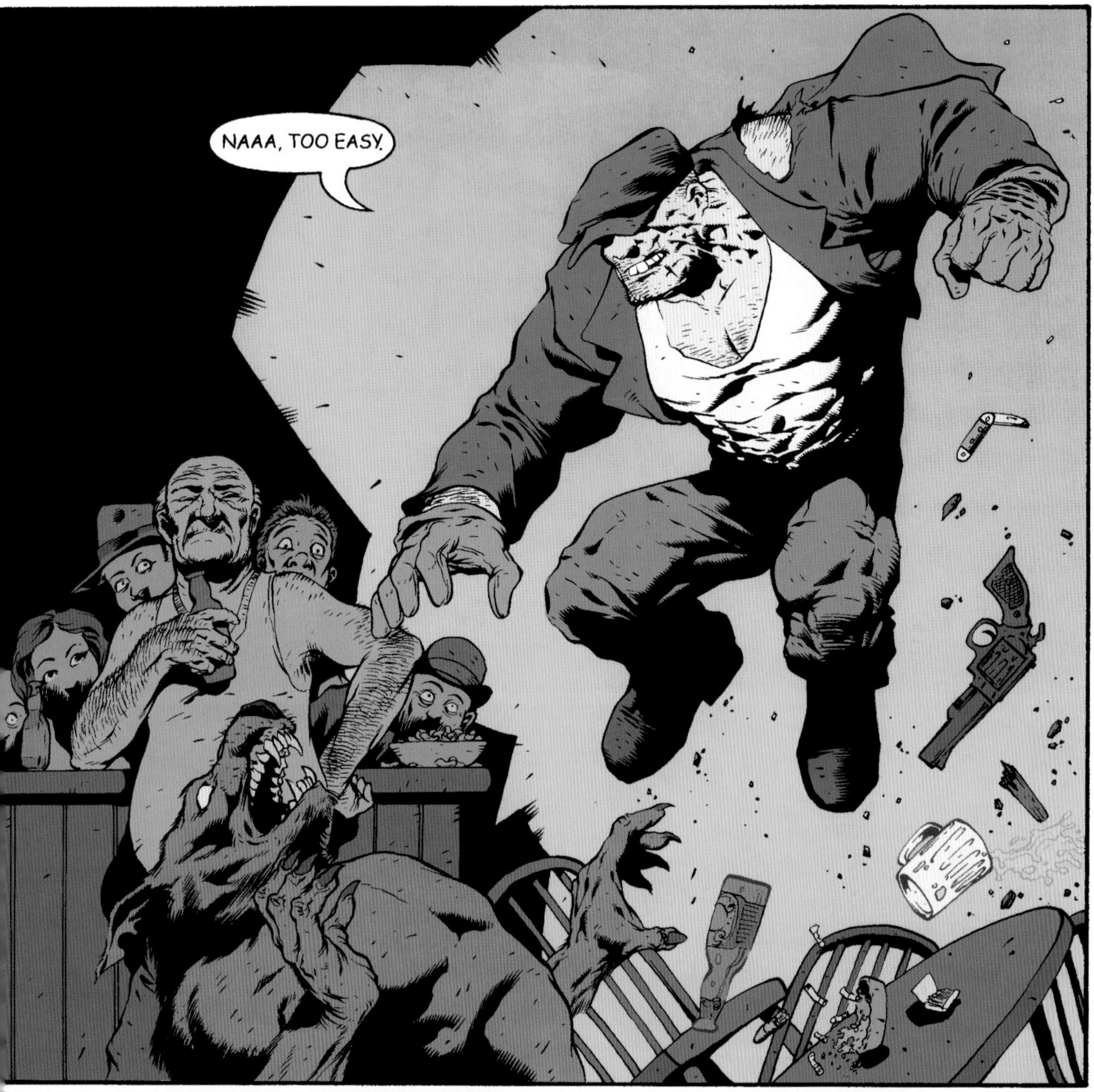
NAAA, TOO EASY.

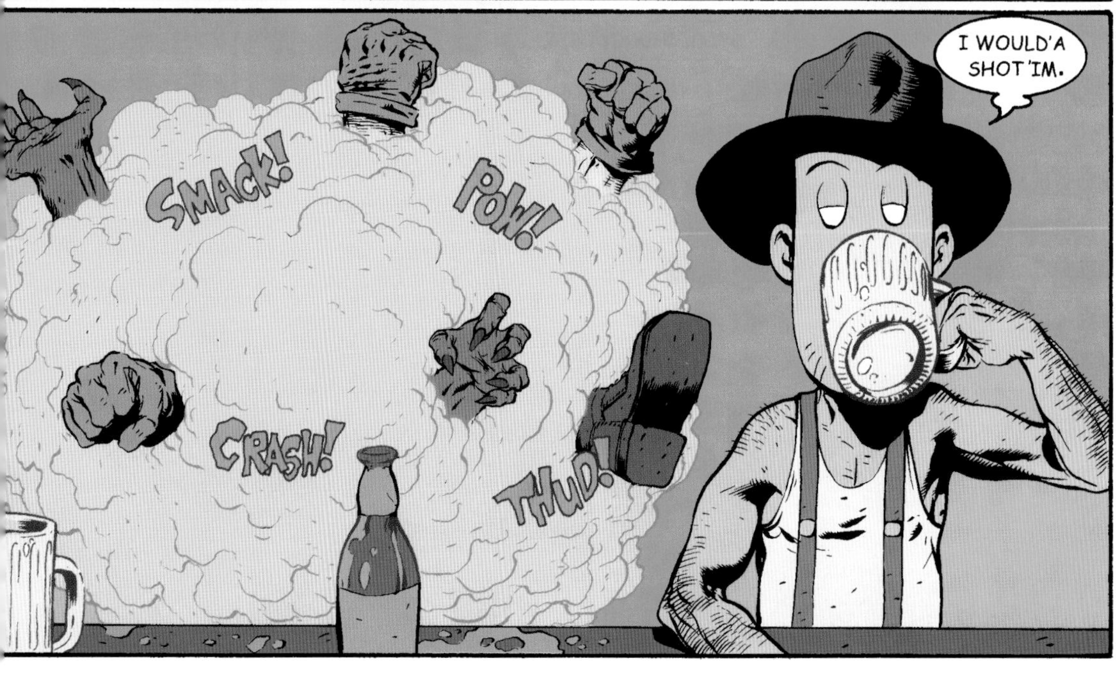
SMACK!
POW!
CRASH!
THUD!
I WOULD'A SHOT 'IM.

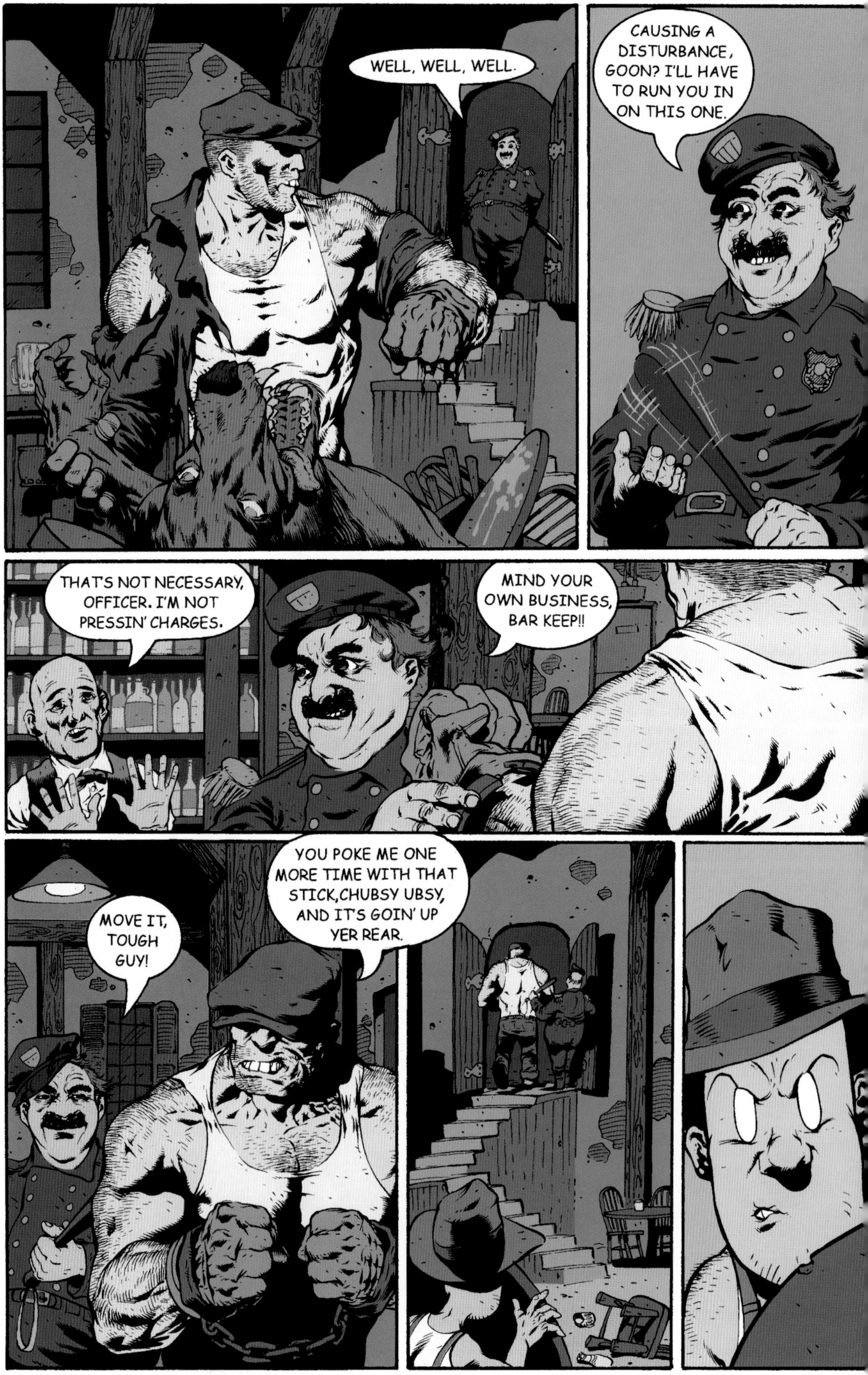
WELL, WELL, WELL.
CAUSING A DISTURBANCE, GOON? I'LL HAVE TO RUN YOU IN ON THIS ONE.
THAT'S NOT NECESSARY, OFFICER. I'M NOT PRESSIN' CHARGES.
MIND YOUR OWN BUSINESS, BAR KEEP!!
MOVE IT, TOUGH GUY!
YOU POKE ME ONE MORE TIME WITH THAT STICK,CHUBSY UBSY, AND IT'S GOIN' UP YER REAR.

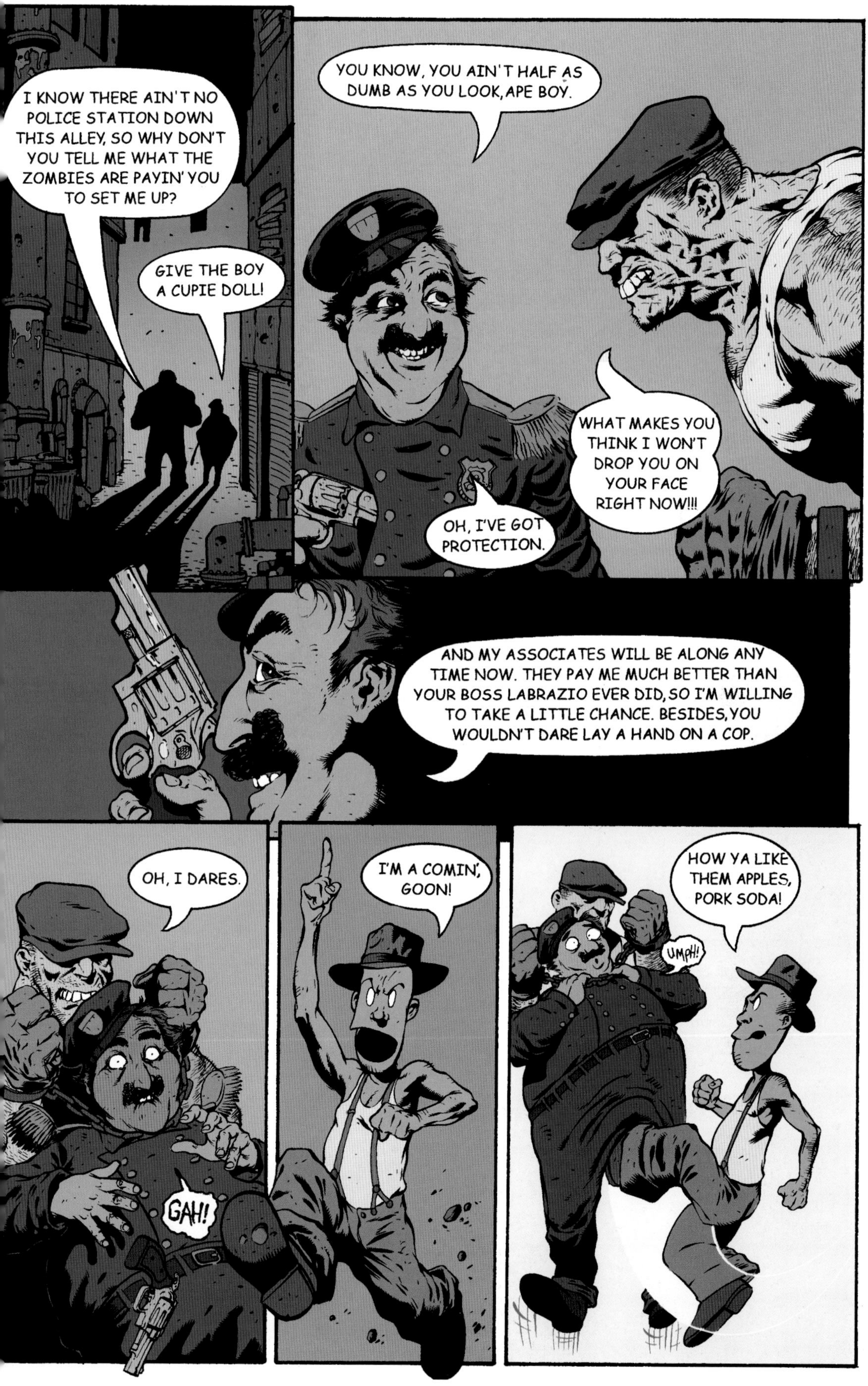
I KNOW THERE AIN'T NO POLICE STATION DOWN THIS ALLEY, SO WHY DON'T YOU TELL ME WHAT THE ZOMBIES ARE PAYIN' YOU TO SET ME UP?
GIVE THE BOY A CUPIE DOLL!
YOU KNOW, YOU AIN'T HALF AS DUMB AS YOU LOOK, APE BOY.
WHAT MAKES YOU THINK I WON'T DROP YOU ON YOUR FACE RIGHT NOW!!!
OH, I'VE GOT PROTECTION.
AND MY ASSOCIATES WILL BE ALONG ANY TIME NOW. THEY PAY ME MUCH BETTER THAN YOUR BOSS LABRAZIO EVER DID, SO I'M WILLING TO TAKE A LITTLE CHANCE. BESIDES, YOU WOULDN'T DARE LAY A HAND ON A COP.
OH, I DARES.
GAH!
I'M A COMIN', GOON!
HOW YA LIKE THEM APPLES, PORK SODA!
UMPH!

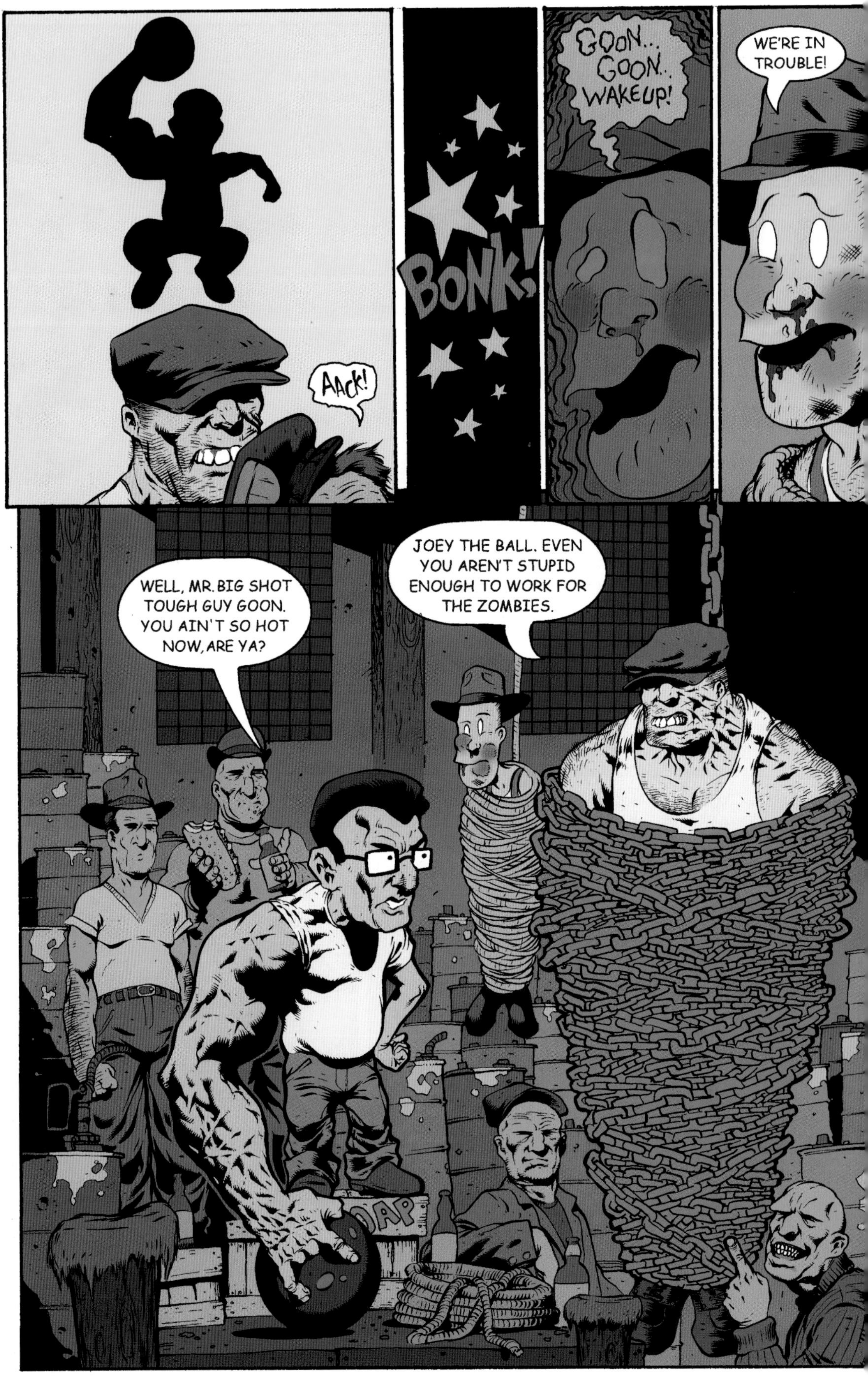
AACK!
BONK!
GOON... GOON.. WAKEUP!
WE'RE IN TROUBLE!
WELL, MR. BIG SHOT TOUGH GUY GOON. YOU AIN'T SO HOT NOW, ARE YA?
JOEY THE BALL. EVEN YOU AREN'T STUPID ENOUGH TO WORK FOR THE ZOMBIES.

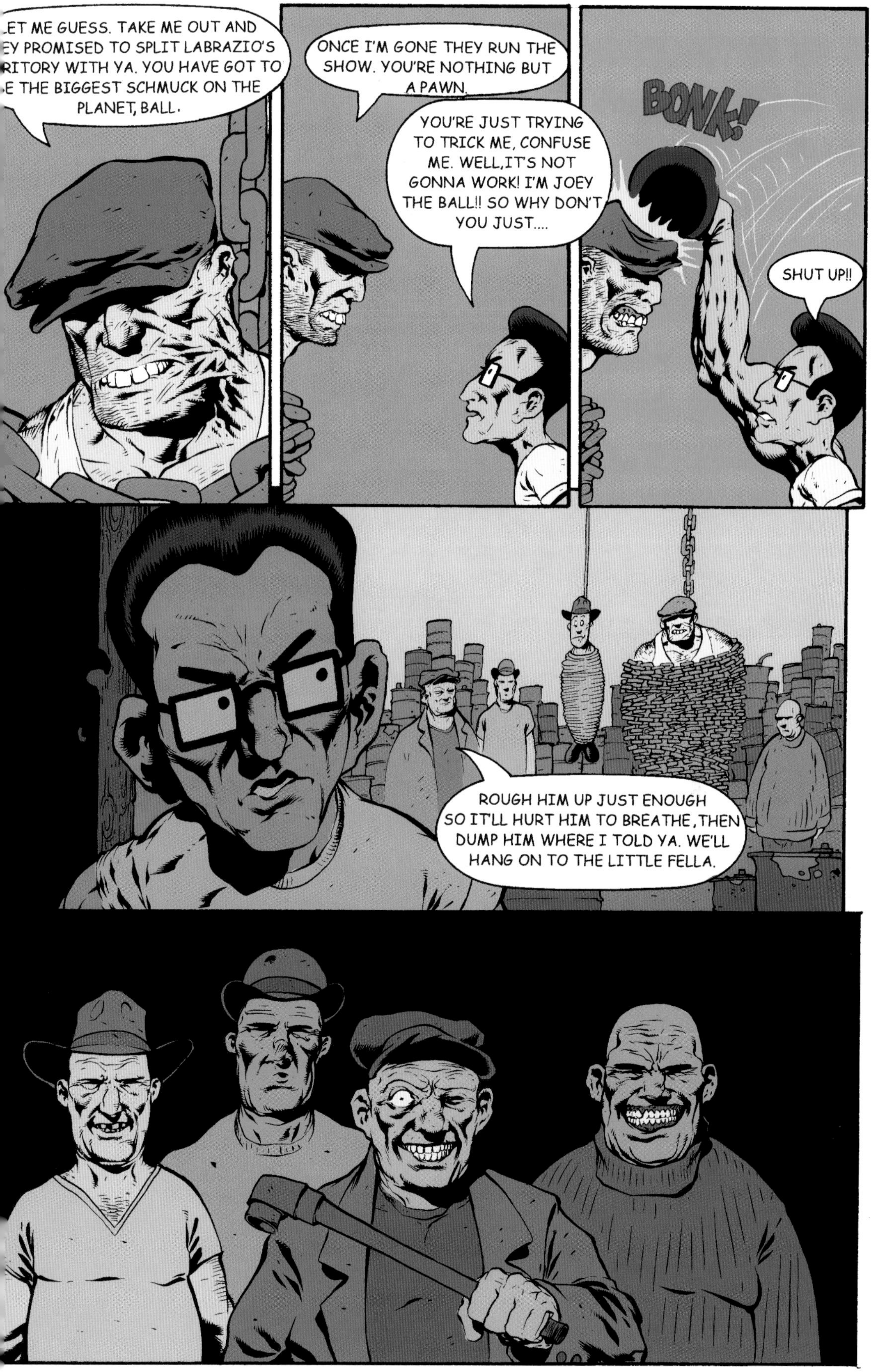
ET ME GUESS. TAKE ME OUT AND EY PROMISED TO SPLIT LABRAZIO'S RITORY WITH YA. YOU HAVE GOT TO E THE BIGGEST SCHMUCK ON THE PLANET, BALL.
ONCE I'M GONE THEY RUN THE SHOW. YOU'RE NOTHING BUT A PAWN.
YOU'RE JUST TRYING TO TRICK ME, CONFUSE ME. WELL, IT'S NOT GONNA WORK! I'M JOEY THE BALL!! SO WHY DON'T YOU JUST....
BONK!
SHUT UP!!
ROUGH HIM UP JUST ENOUGH SO IT'LL HURT HIM TO BREATHE, THEN DUMP HIM WHERE I TOLD YA. WE'LL HANG ON TO THE LITTLE FELLA.

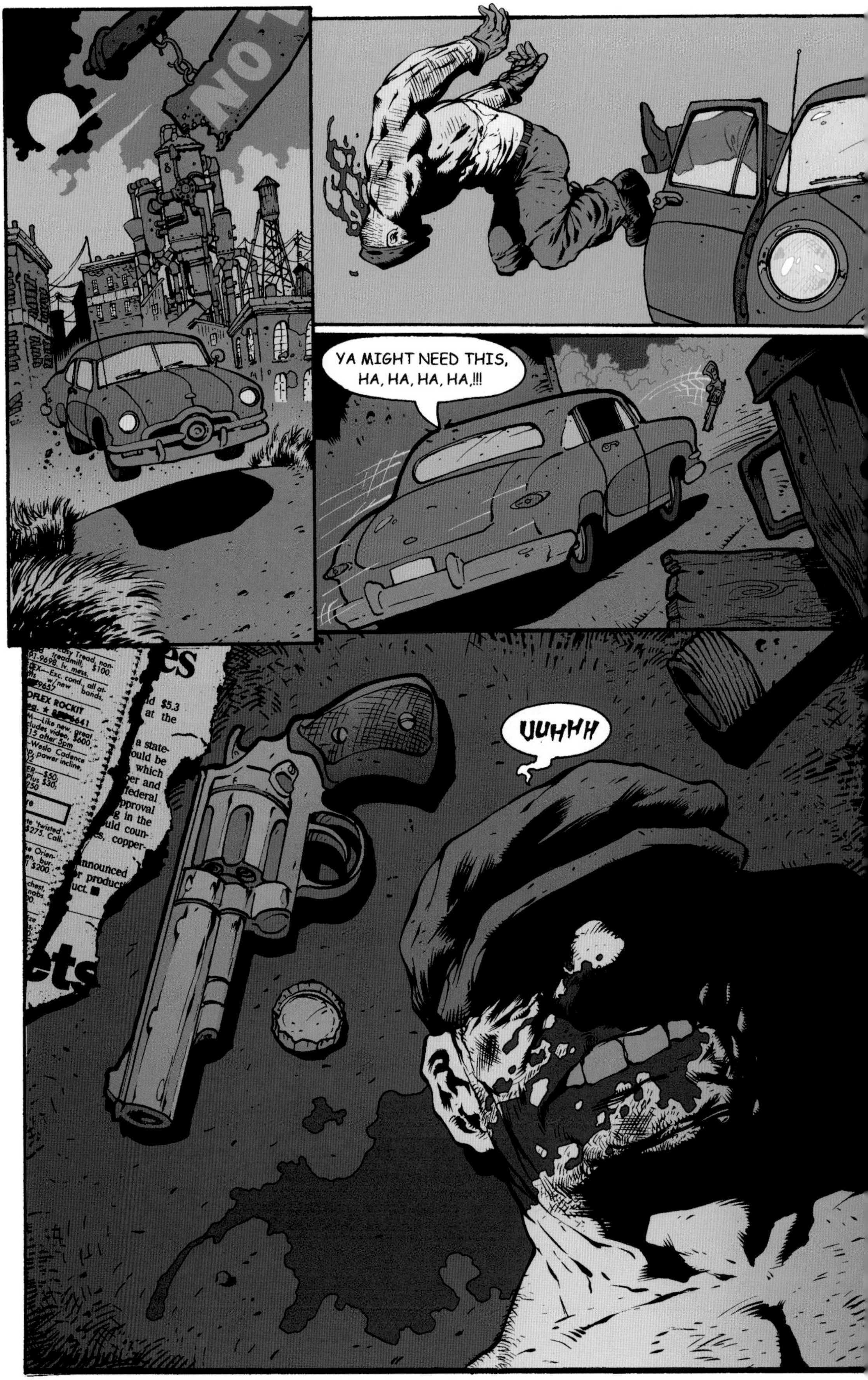
YA MIGHT NEED THIS, HA, HA, HA, HA,!!!
UUHHH

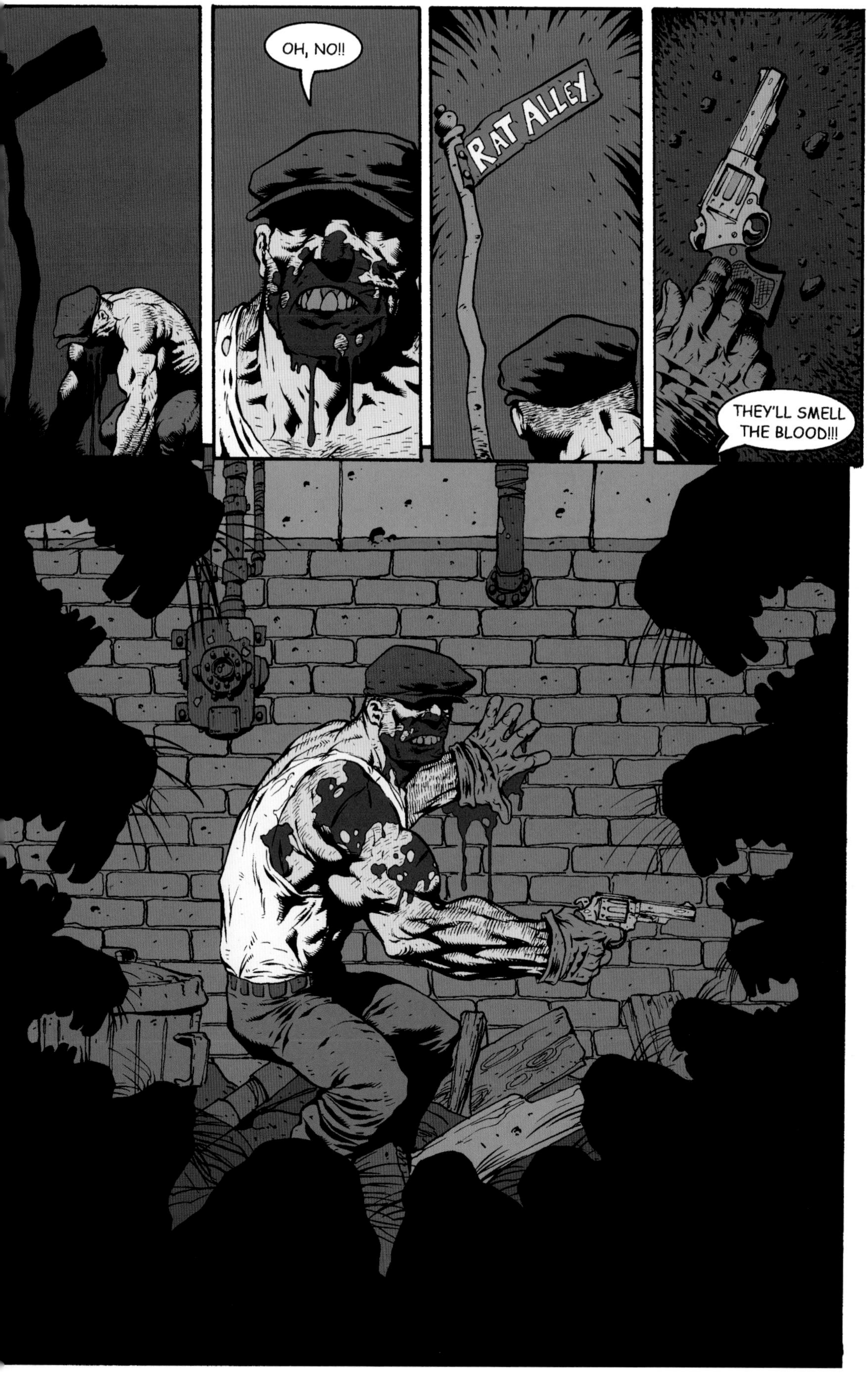
OH, NO!!
RAT ALLEY
THEY'LL SMELL THE BLOOD!!!

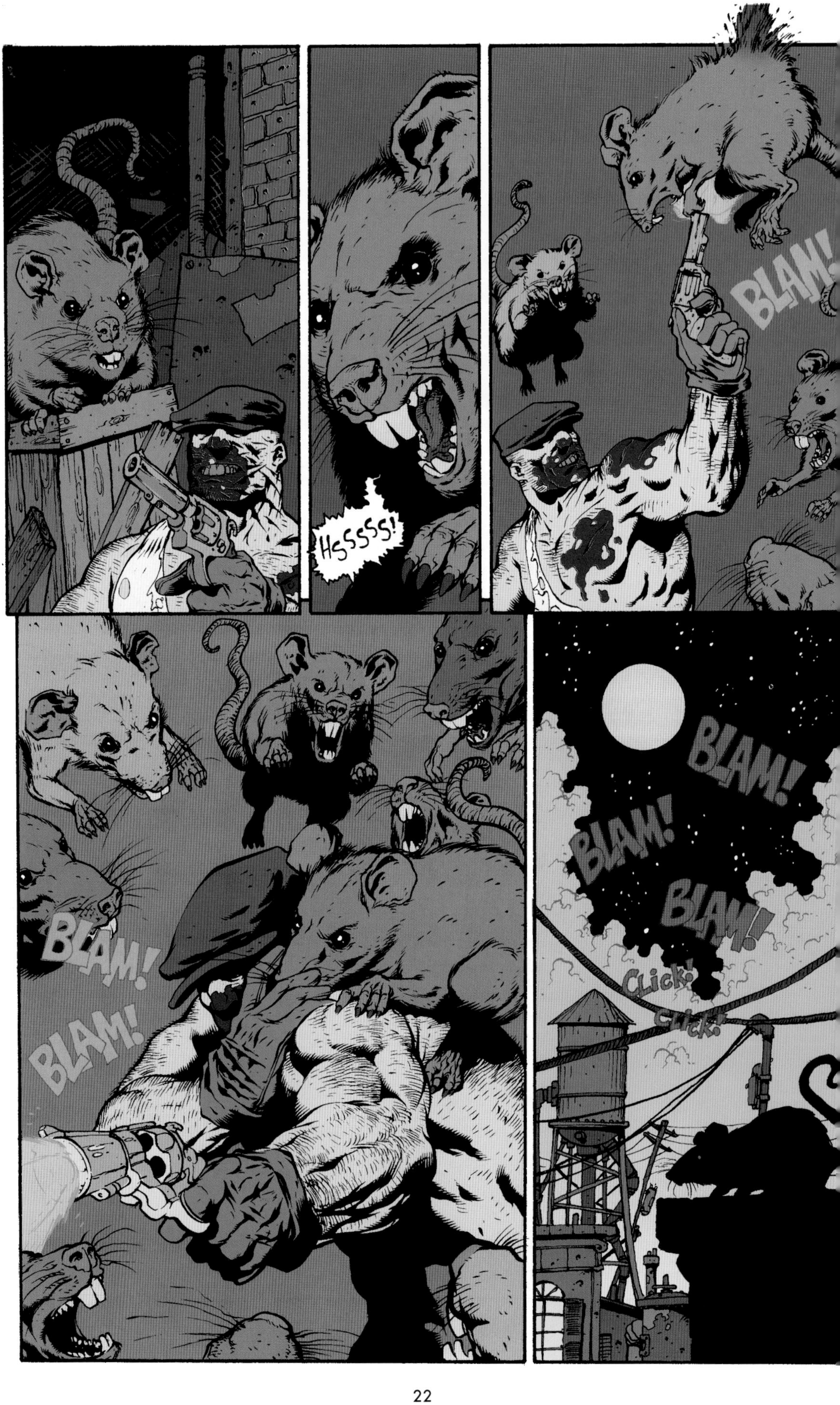
HSSSSS!
BLAM!
BLAM!
BLAM!
BLAM!
BLAM!
BLAM!
CLICK!
CLICK!

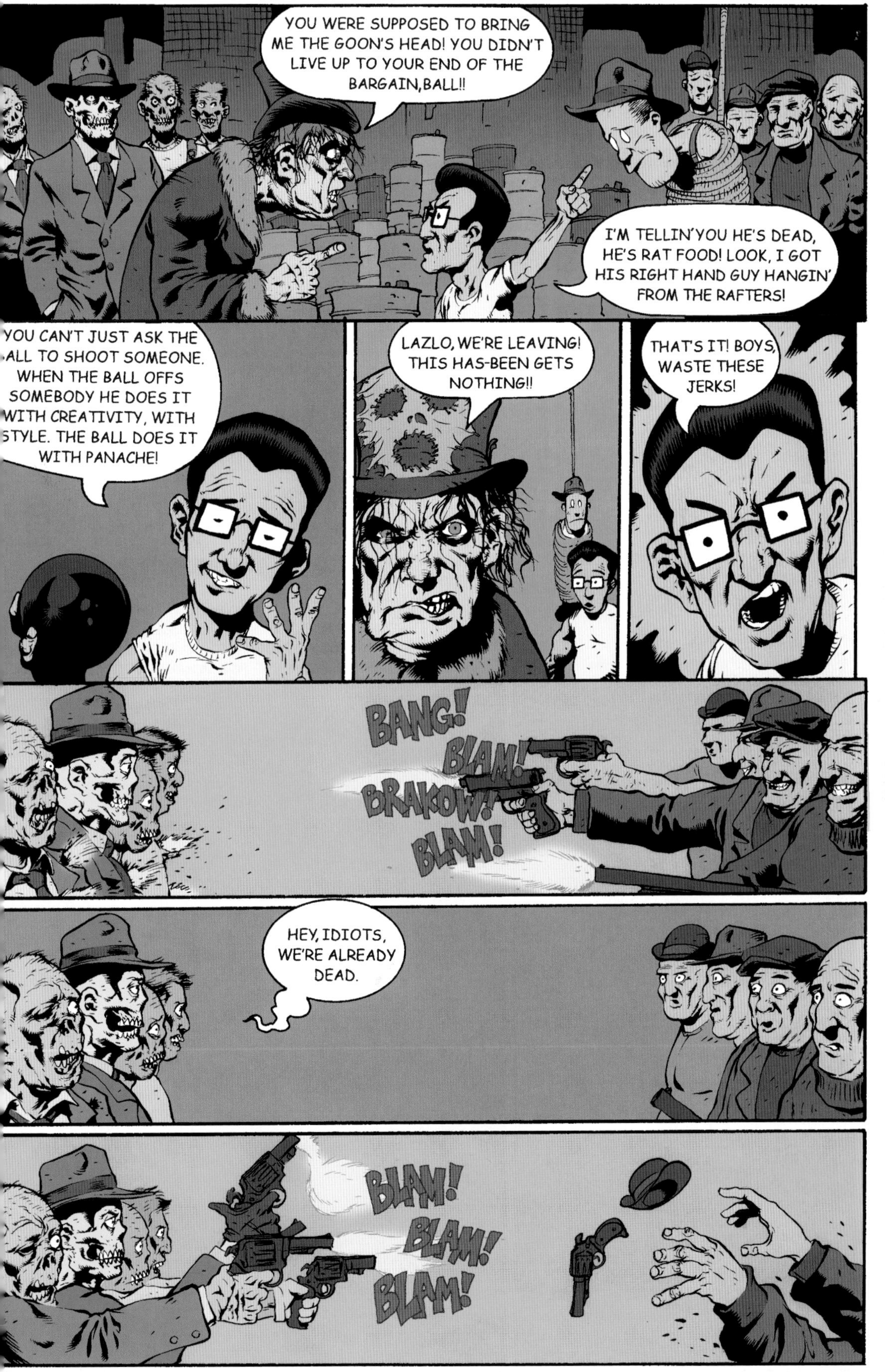
YOU WERE SUPPOSED TO BRING ME THE GOON'S HEAD! YOU DIDN'T LIVE UP TO YOUR END OF THE BARGAIN, BALL!!
I'M TELLIN' YOU HE'S DEAD, HE'S RAT FOOD! LOOK, I GOT HIS RIGHT HAND GUY HANGIN' FROM THE RAFTERS!
YOU CAN'T JUST ASK THE BALL TO SHOOT SOMEONE. WHEN THE BALL OFFS SOMEBODY HE DOES IT WITH CREATIVITY, WITH STYLE. THE BALL DOES IT WITH PANACHE!
LAZLO, WE'RE LEAVING! THIS HAS-BEEN GETS NOTHING!!
THAT'S IT! BOYS, WASTE THESE JERKS!
BANG!
BLAM!
BRAKOW!
BLAM!
HEY, IDIOTS, WE'RE ALREADY DEAD.
BLAM!
BLAM!
BLAM!

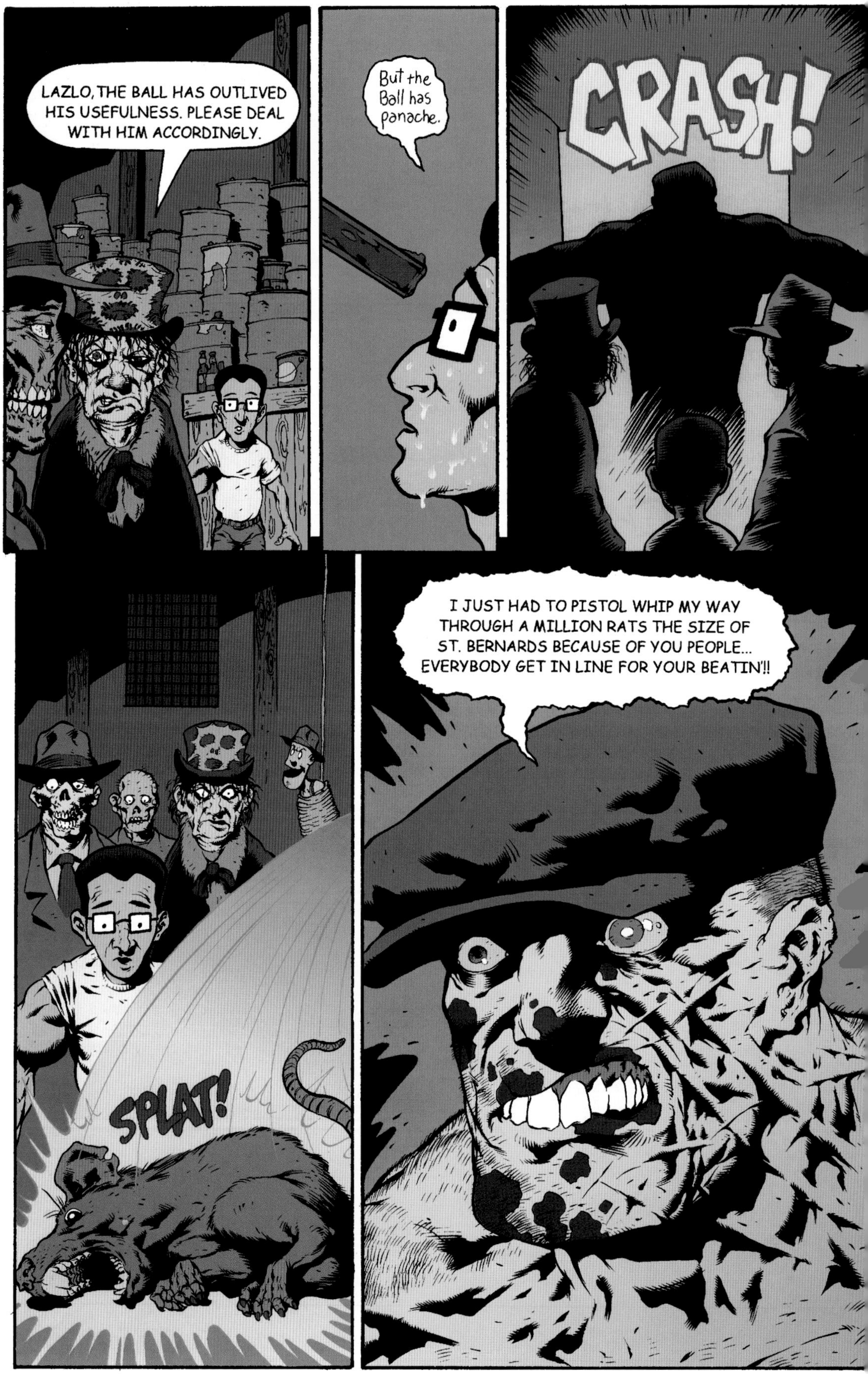

LAZLO, THE BALL HAS OUTLIVED HIS USEFULNESS. PLEASE DEAL WITH HIM ACCORDINGLY.
But the Ball has panache.
CRASH!
SPLAT!
I JUST HAD TO PISTOL WHIP MY WAY THROUGH A MILLION RATS THE SIZE OF ST. BERNARDS BECAUSE OF YOU PEOPLE... EVERYBODY GET IN LINE FOR YOUR BEATIN'!!

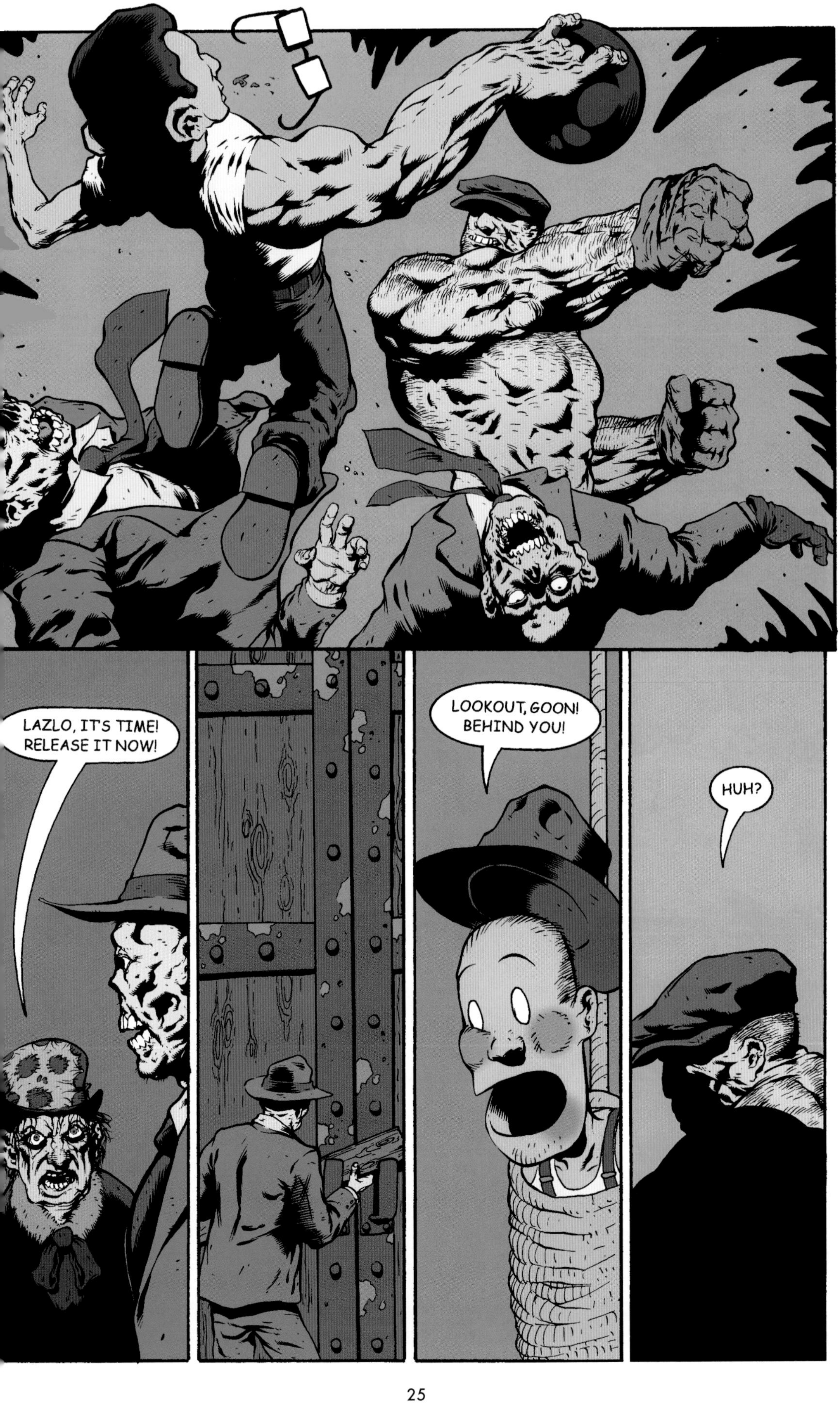
LAZLO, IT'S TIME! RELEASE IT NOW!
LOOKOUT, GOON! BEHIND YOU!
HUH?

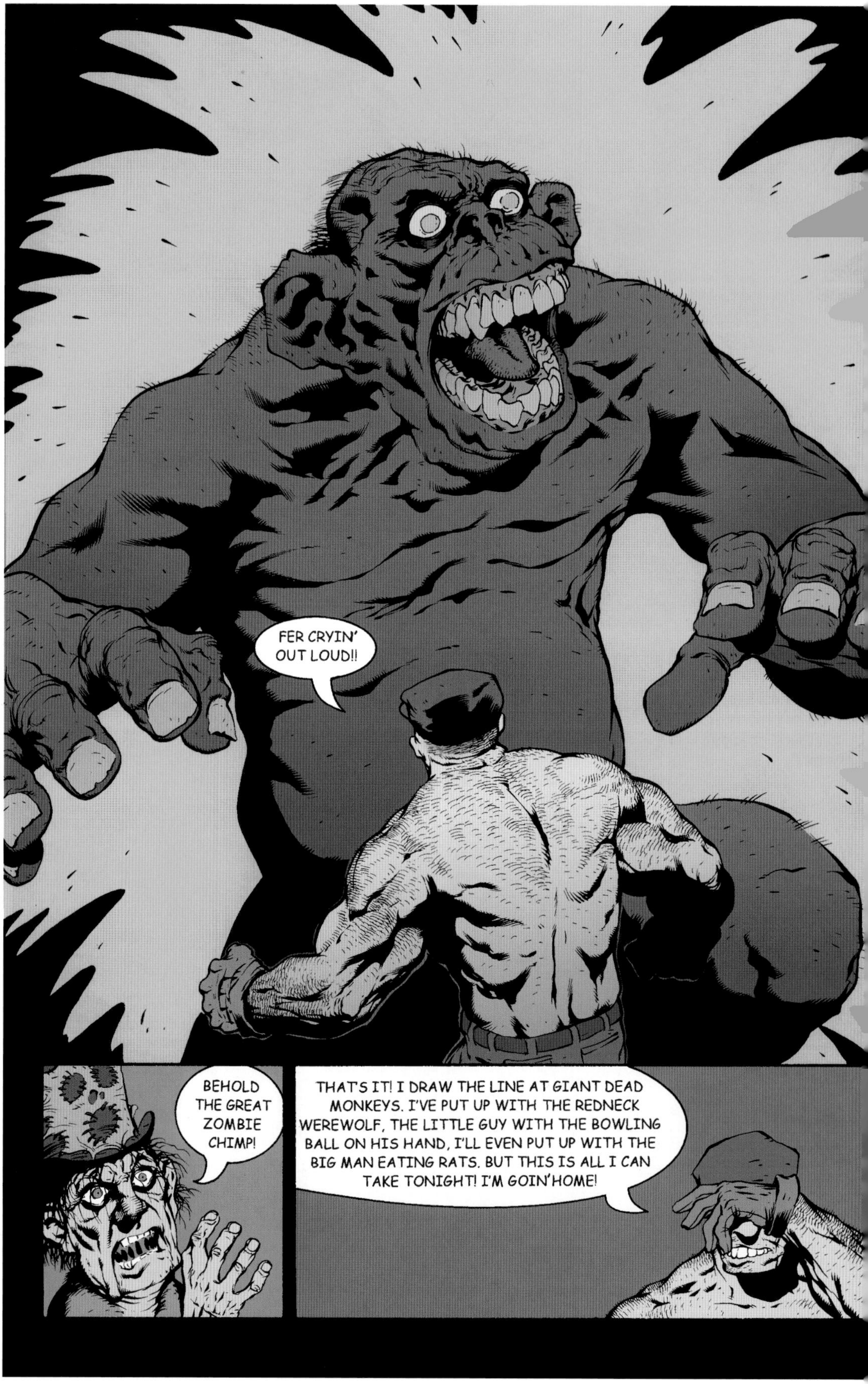
FER CRYIN' OUT LOUD!!
BEHOLD THE GREAT ZOMBIE CHIMP!
THAT'S IT! I DRAW THE LINE AT GIANT DEAD MONKEYS. I'VE PUT UP WITH THE REDNECK WEREWOLF, THE LITTLE GUY WITH THE BOWLING BALL ON HIS HAND, I'LL EVEN PUT UP WITH THE BIG MAN EATING RATS. BUT THIS IS ALL I CAN TAKE TONIGHT! I'M GOIN'HOME!

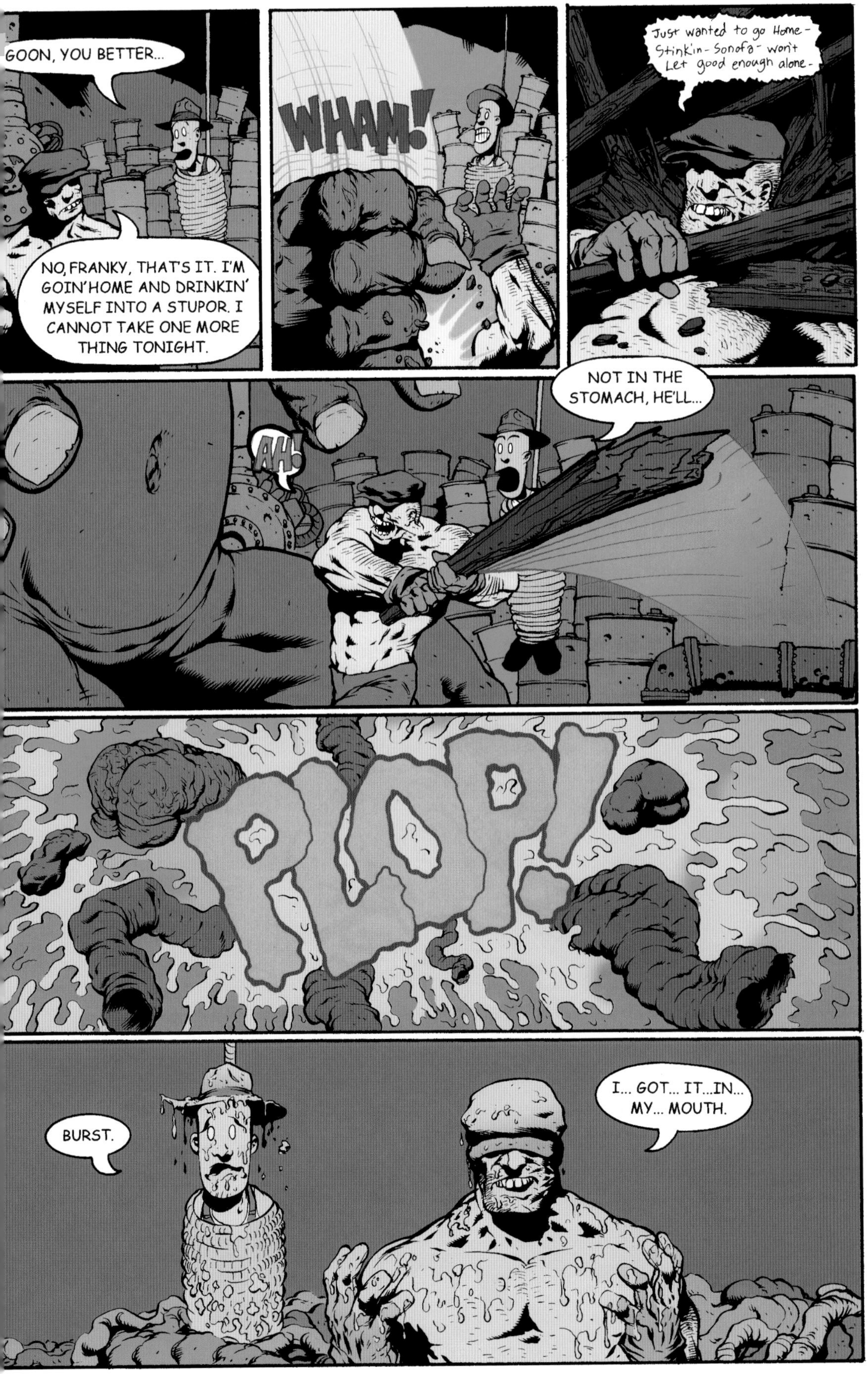
GOON, YOU BETTER...
NO, FRANKY, THAT'S IT. I'M GOIN' HOME AND DRINKIN' MYSELF INTO A STUPOR. I CANNOT TAKE ONE MORE THING TONIGHT.
WHAM!
Just wanted to go Home - Stinkin - Sonofa - won't Let good enough alone -
AH!
NOT IN THE STOMACH, HE'LL...
PLOP!
BURST.
I... GOT... IT...IN... MY... MOUTH.

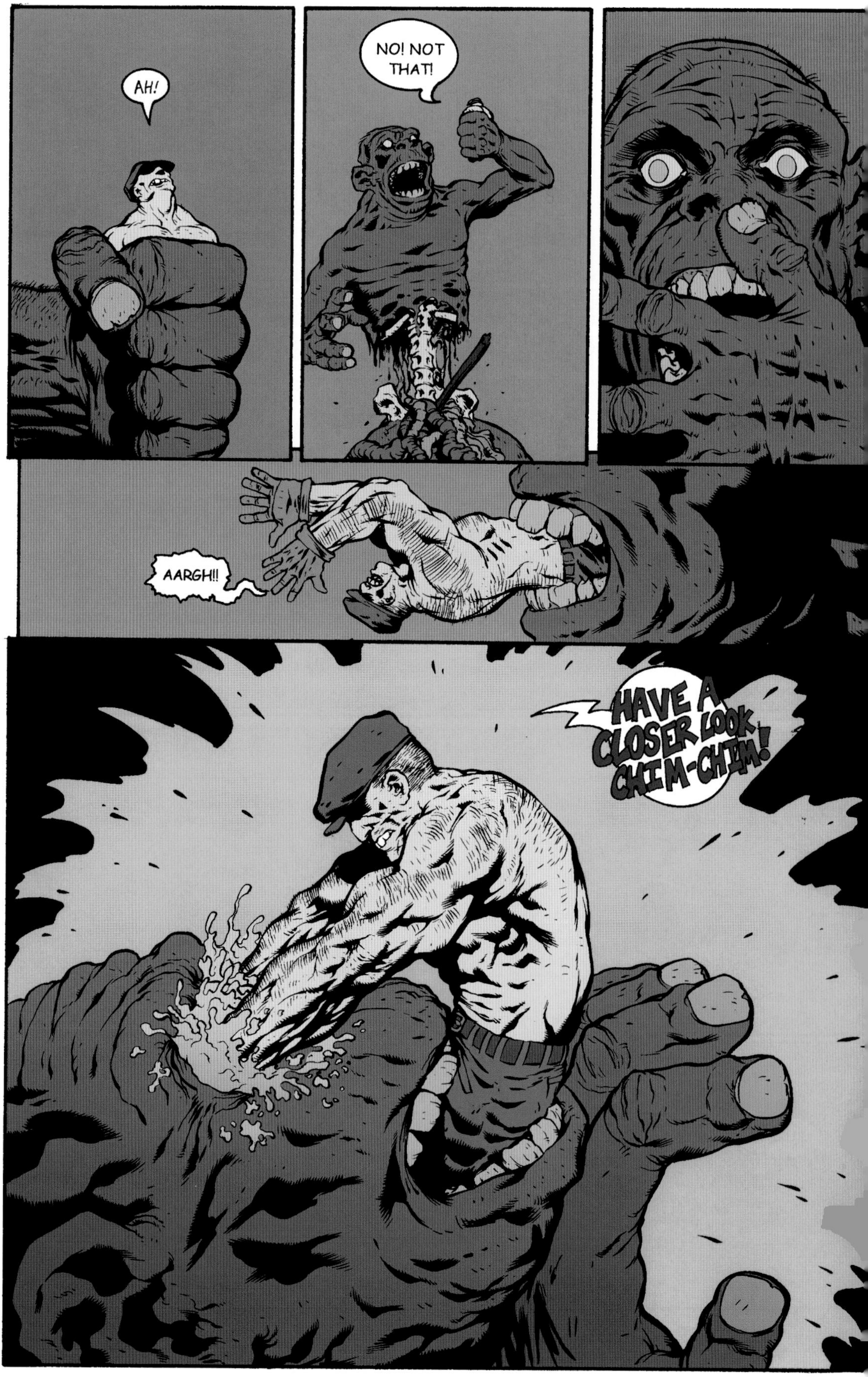
AH!
NO! NOT THAT!
AARGH!!
HAVE A CLOSER LOOK, CHIM-CHIM!

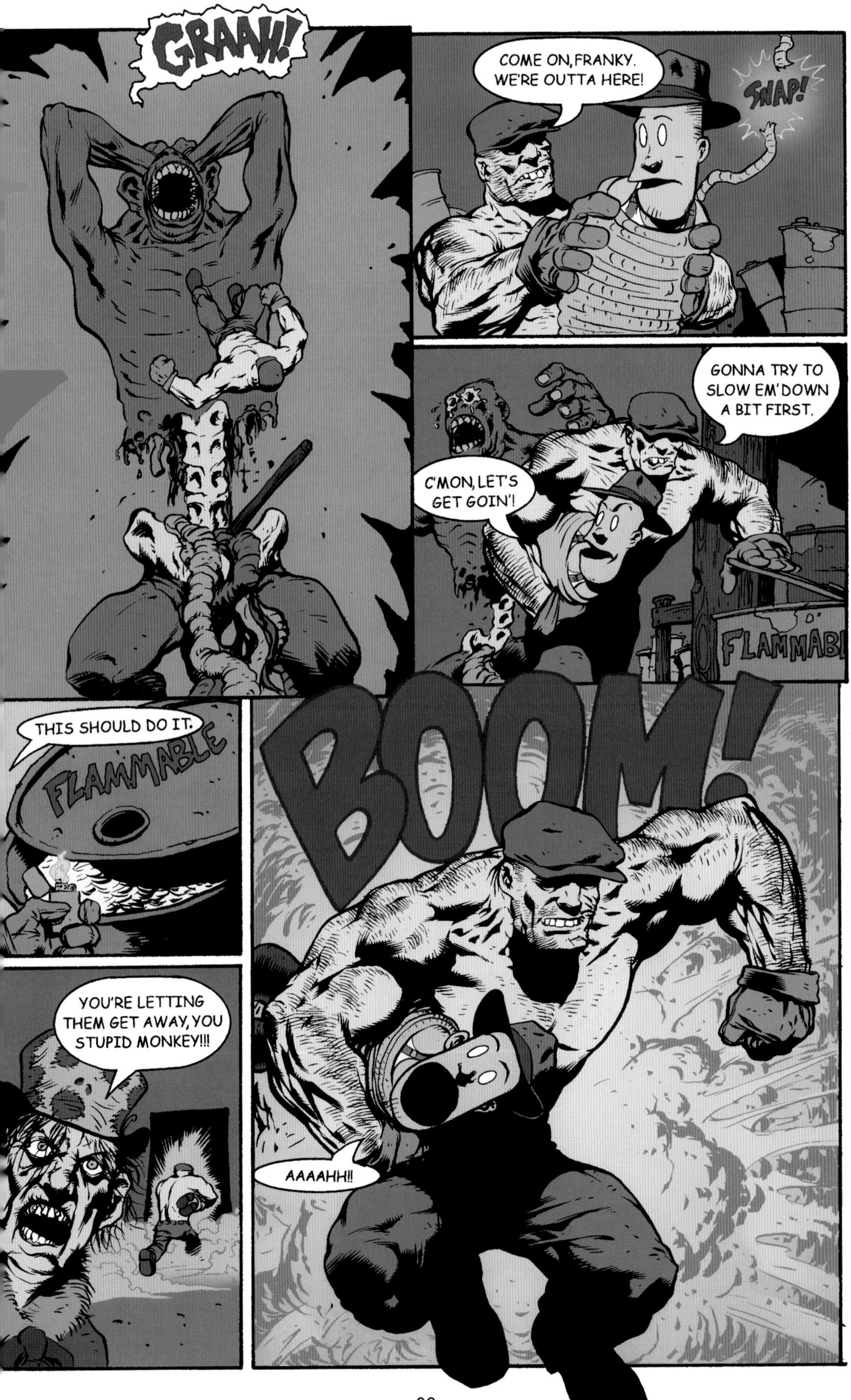
GRAAH!
COME ON, FRANKY. WE'RE OUTTA HERE!
SNAP!
GONNA TRY TO SLOW EM' DOWN A BIT FIRST.
C'MON, LET'S GET GOIN'!
FLAMMABL
THIS SHOULD DO IT.
FLAMMABLE
YOU'RE LETTING THEM GET AWAY, YOU STUPID MONKEY!!!
BOOM!
AAAAHH!!

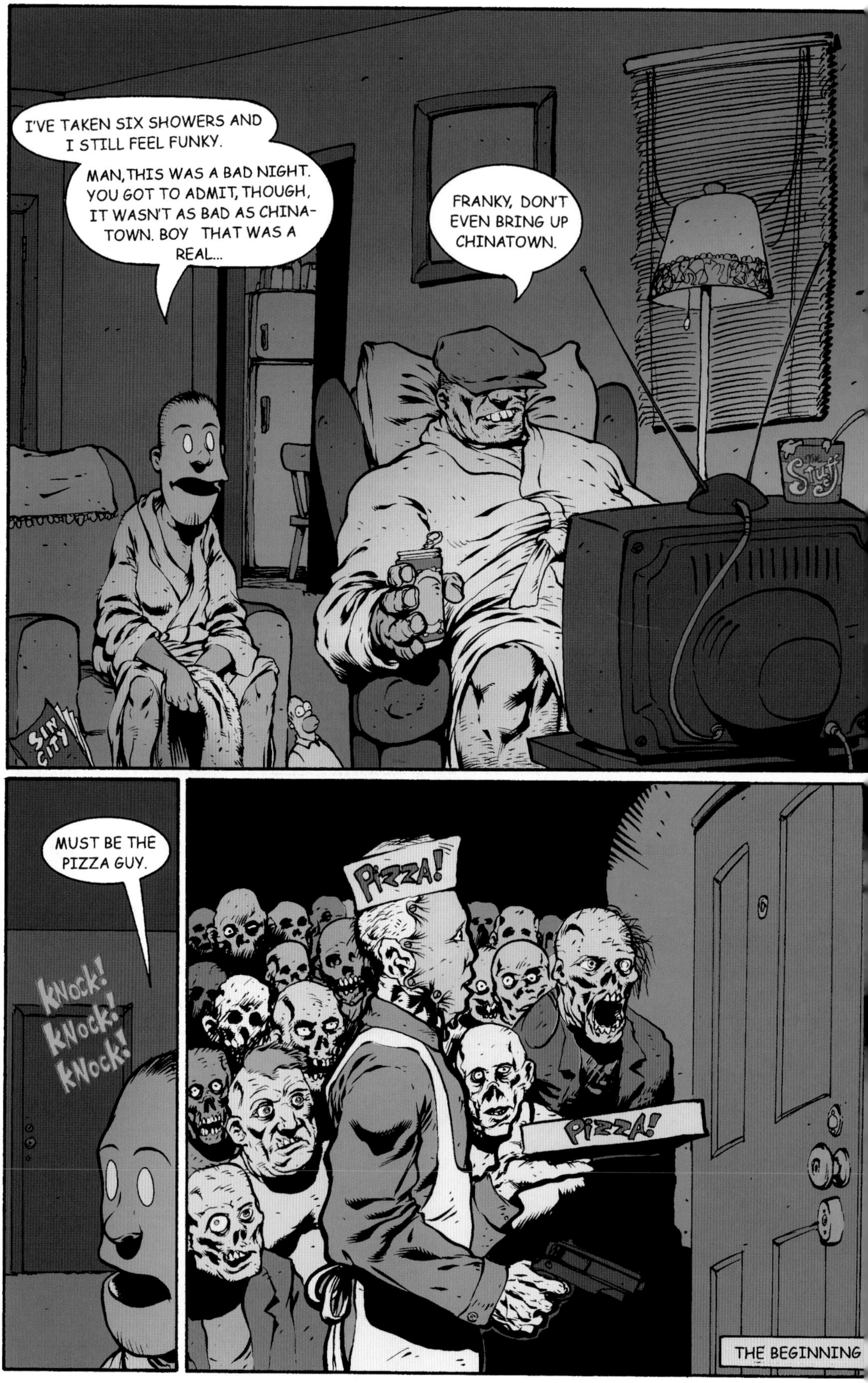
I'VE TAKEN SIX SHOWERS AND I STILL FEEL FUNKY.
MAN, THIS WAS A BAD NIGHT. YOU GOT TO ADMIT, THOUGH, IT WASN'T AS BAD AS CHINA-TOWN. BOY THAT WAS A REAL...
FRANKY, DON'T EVEN BRING UP CHINATOWN.
Stuff
SIN CITY
MUST BE THE PIZZA GUY.
KNOCK! KNOCK! KNOCK!
PIZZA!
PIZZA!
THE BEGINNING

# CHAPTER 2

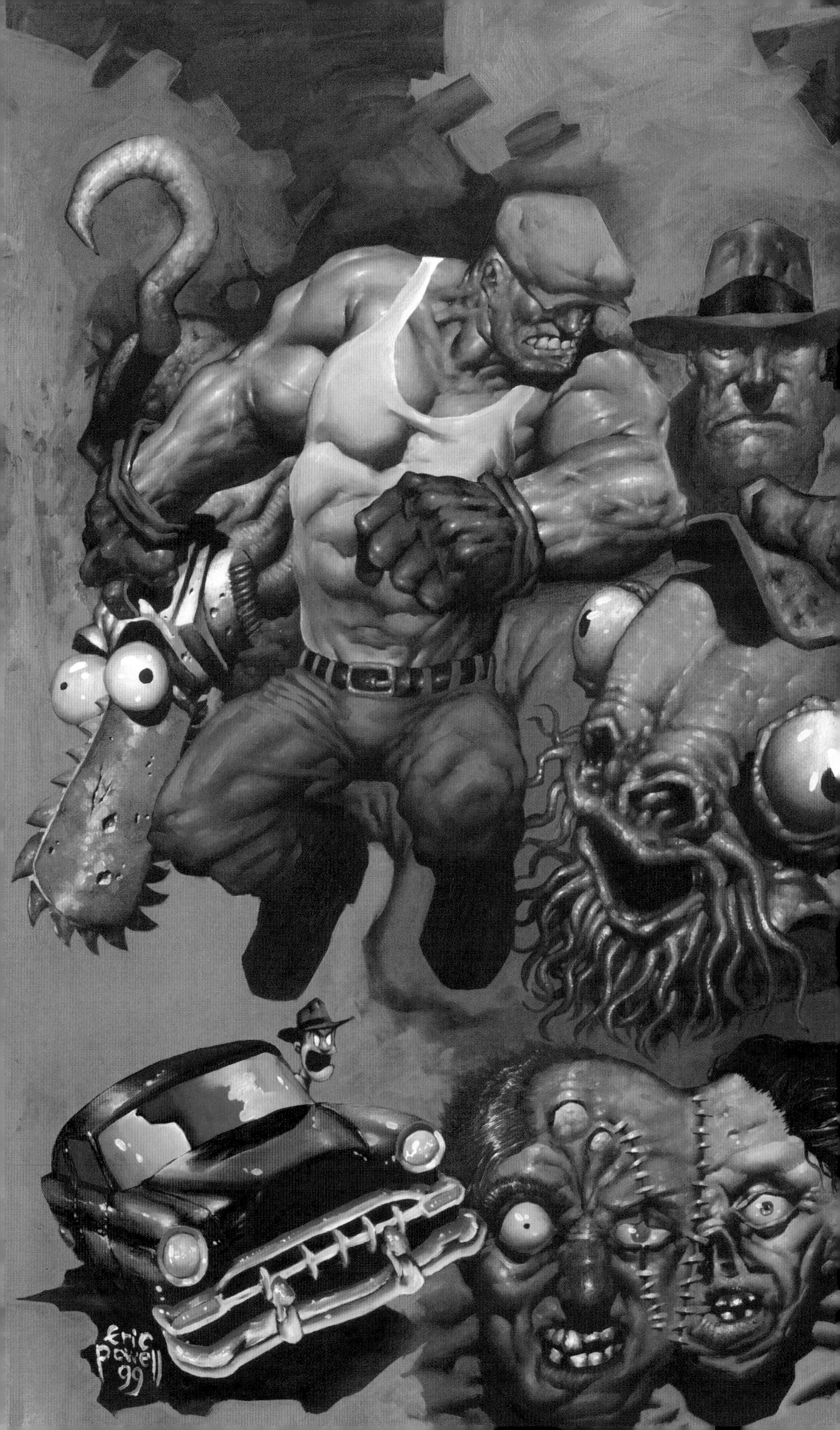
Eric
Powell
99

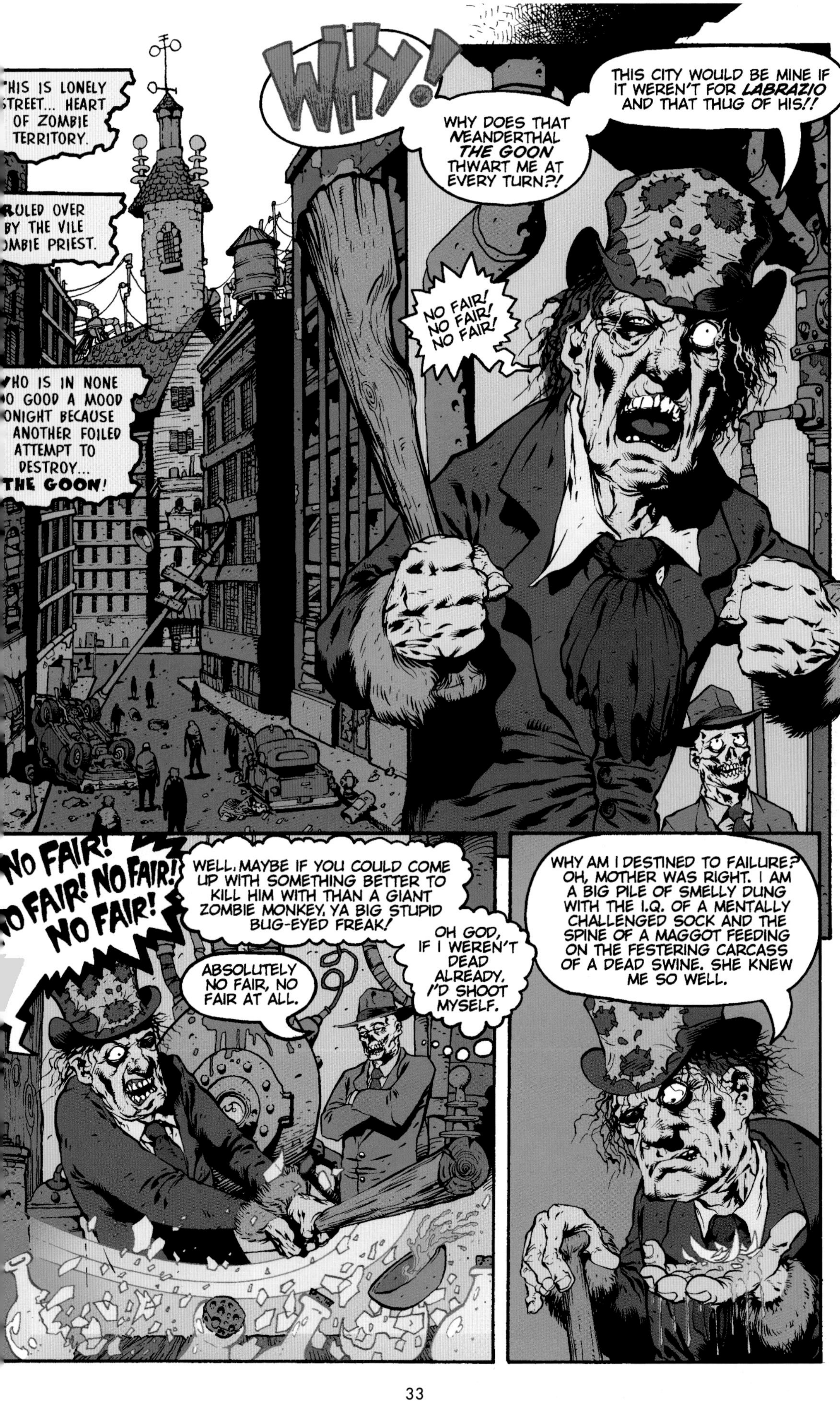

HIS IS LONELY TREET... HEART OF ZOMBIE TERRITORY.
RULED OVER BY THE VILE MBIE PRIEST.
HO IS IN NONE O GOOD A MOOD ONIGHT BECAUSE ANOTHER FOILED ATTEMPT TO DESTROY... THE GOON!
WHY!
WHY DOES THAT NEANDERTHAL THE GOON THWART ME AT EVERY TURN?!
THIS CITY WOULD BE MINE IF IT WEREN'T FOR LABRAZIO AND THAT THUG OF HIS!!
NO FAIR! NO FAIR! NO FAIR!
NO FAIR! O FAIR! NO FAIR! NO FAIR!
WELL, MAYBE IF YOU COULD COME UP WITH SOMETHING BETTER TO KILL HIM WITH THAN A GIANT ZOMBIE MONKEY, YA BIG STUPID BUG-EYED FREAK!
ABSOLUTELY NO FAIR, NO FAIR AT ALL.
OH GOD, IF I WEREN'T DEAD ALREADY, I'D SHOOT MYSELF.
WHY AM I DESTINED TO FAILURE? OH, MOTHER WAS RIGHT. I AM A BIG PILE OF SMELLY DUNG WITH THE I.Q. OF A MENTALLY CHALLENGED SOCK AND THE SPINE OF A MAGGOT FEEDING ON THE FESTERING CARCASS OF A DEAD SWINE. SHE KNEW ME SO WELL.

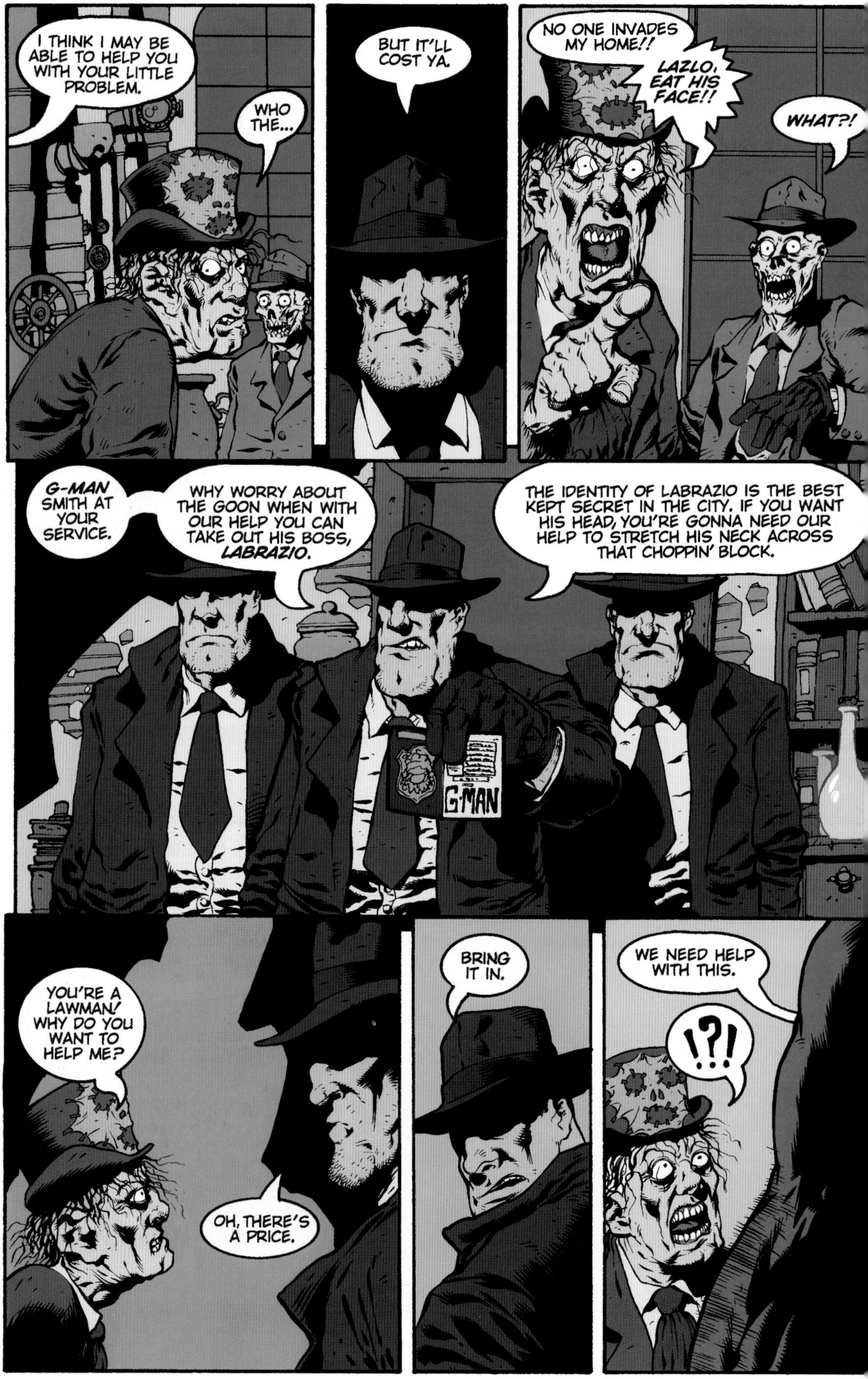
I THINK I MAY BE ABLE TO HELP YOU WITH YOUR LITTLE PROBLEM.
WHO THE...
BUT IT'LL COST YA.
NO ONE INVADES MY HOME!!
LAZLO, EAT HIS FACE!!
WHAT?!
G-MAN SMITH AT YOUR SERVICE.
WHY WORRY ABOUT THE GOON WHEN WITH OUR HELP YOU CAN TAKE OUT HIS BOSS, LABRAZIO.
THE IDENTITY OF LABRAZIO IS THE BEST KEPT SECRET IN THE CITY. IF YOU WANT HIS HEAD, YOU'RE GONNA NEED OUR HELP TO STRETCH HIS NECK ACROSS THAT CHOPPIN' BLOCK.
G-MAN
YOU'RE A LAWMAN! WHY DO YOU WANT TO HELP ME?
OH, THERE'S A PRICE.
BRING IT IN.
WE NEED HELP WITH THIS.
!?!

AND ON THE OTHER SIDE OF THE CITY...

YOU GUYS AIN'T GETTIN' NUTTIN' OUTTA US!

WE BEEN HOG TIED BY TUFFER 'AN 'U, AND WE AIN'T NEVER SQUEALED!

YEAH! YOU MUGS DON'T SCARE US NONE.

HEY, FINKLE, YOU REMEMBER WHEN ZOOKO HAD HIS BOYS TRY TA DROWN US IN THE RIVER?

HA! HA! HA! HA!

YEAH, CHARLIE! FOR STEALIN' HIS TAKE!

HA! HA! HA!

AND REMEMBER WHEN YOU STOLE LEWY'S NEW CAR, AND HE SHOT YOUR MOTHER IN THE FACE?!

HA! HA! HA! HA! HA! HA!

HA! HA! HA!

HEY!

SO YOU SEE, THERE AIN'T NOTHIN' YOU CAN DO TO MAKE US TELL YOU WHERE THAT DROP'S BEING MADE.

WHO SAID WE WANTED ANYTHING OUTTA YA.

WE JUST DO THIS FOR KICKS.

THE FIRST WIVES CLUB

PLAY

STOP

SWEET JESUS NO!!

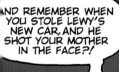

35

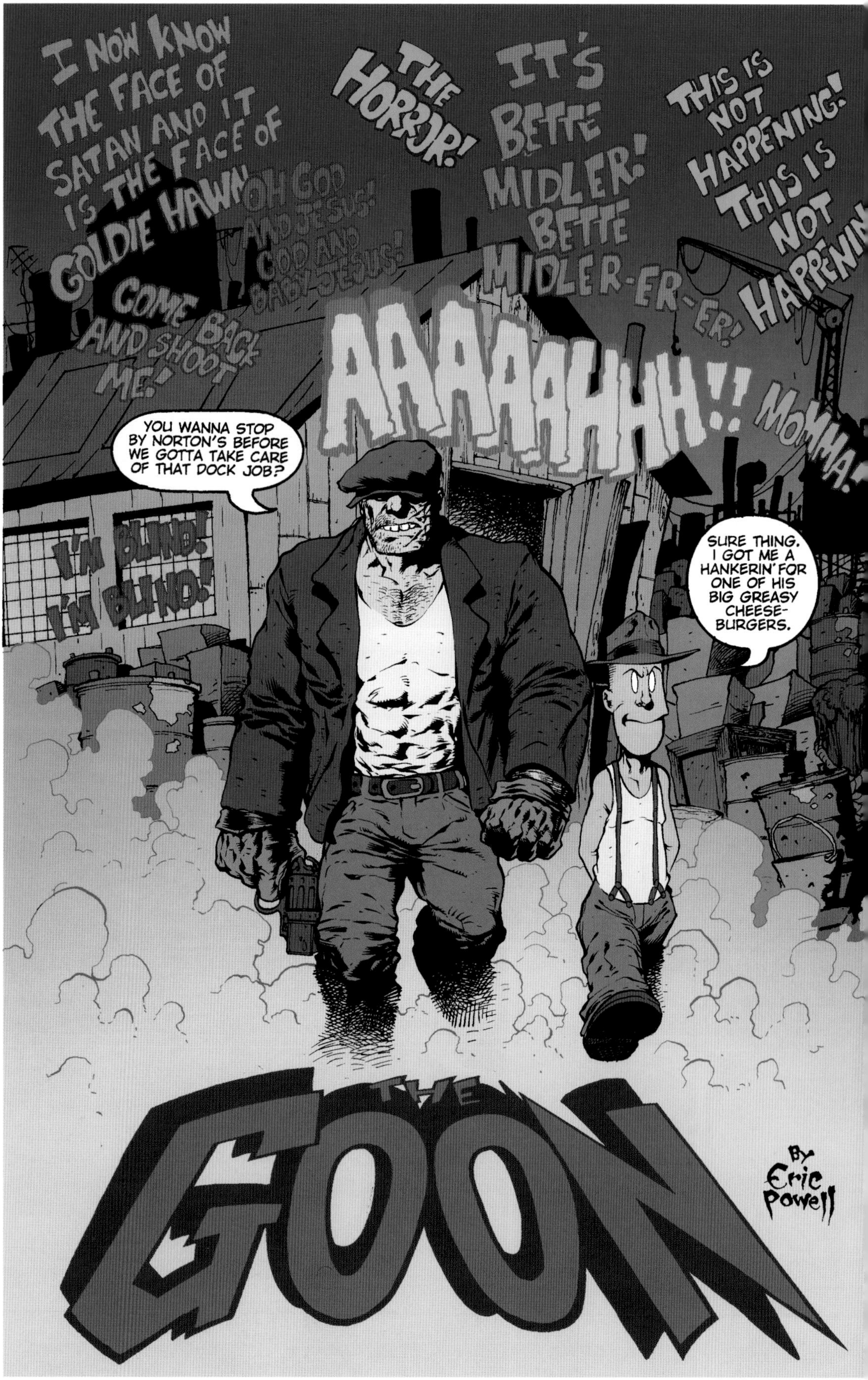
I NOW KNOW THE FACE OF SATAN AND IT IS THE FACE OF GOLDIE HAWN
OH GOD AND JESUS! GOD AND BABY JESUS!
COME BACK AND SHOOT ME!
THE HORROR!
IT'S BETTE MIDLER! BETTE MIDLER-ER-ER!
THIS IS NOT HAPPENING! THIS IS NOT HAPPENIN
AAAAAHHH!!
MOMMA!
YOU WANNA STOP BY NORTON'S BEFORE WE GOTTA TAKE CARE OF THAT DOCK JOB?
I'M BLIND! I'M BLIND!
SURE THING. I GOT ME A HANKERIN' FOR ONE OF HIS BIG GREASY CHEESE-BURGERS.
THE GOON
BY Eric Powell

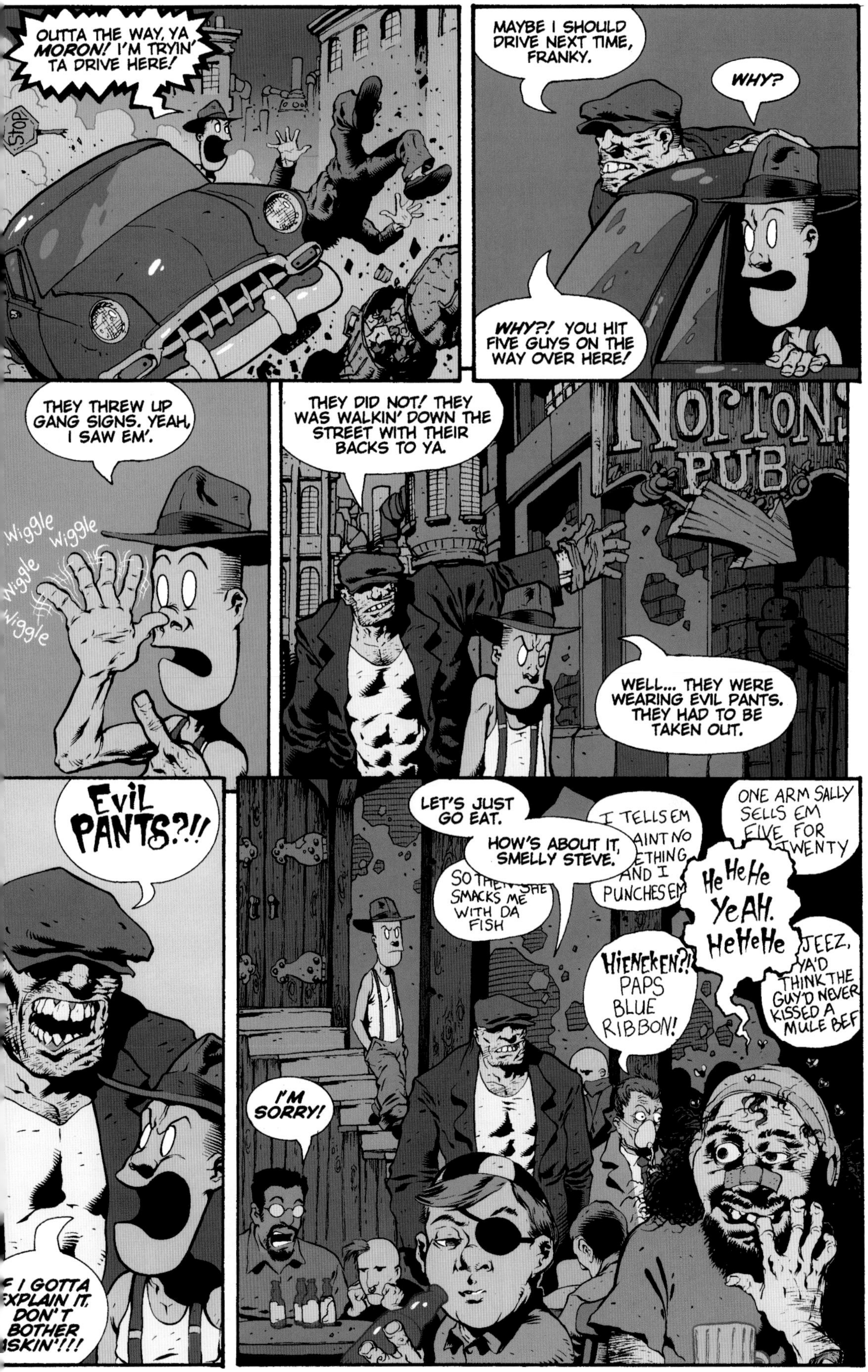

OUTTA THE WAY, YA MORON! I'M TRYIN' TA DRIVE HERE!
STOP
MAYBE I SHOULD DRIVE NEXT TIME, FRANKY.
WHY?
WHY?! YOU HIT FIVE GUYS ON THE WAY OVER HERE!
THEY THREW UP GANG SIGNS. YEAH, I SAW EM'.
wiggle wiggle wiggle wiggle wiggle
THEY DID NOT! THEY WAS WALKIN' DOWN THE STREET WITH THEIR BACKS TO YA.
NORTON'S PUB
WELL... THEY WERE WEARING EVIL PANTS. THEY HAD TO BE TAKEN OUT.
EVIL PANTS?!!
F I GOTTA EXPLAIN IT, DON'T BOTHER ASKIN'!!!
LET'S JUST GO EAT.
HOW'S ABOUT IT, SMELLY STEVE.
SO THEN SHE SMACKS ME WITH DA FISH
I TELLS EM AINT NO ETHING AND I PUNCHES EM
ONE ARM SALLY SELLS EM FIVE FOR TWENTY
He He He YeAH. He He He
JEEZ, YA'D THINK THE GUY'D NEVER KISSED A MULE BEF
HIENEKEN?! PAPS BLUE RIBBON!
I'M SORRY!

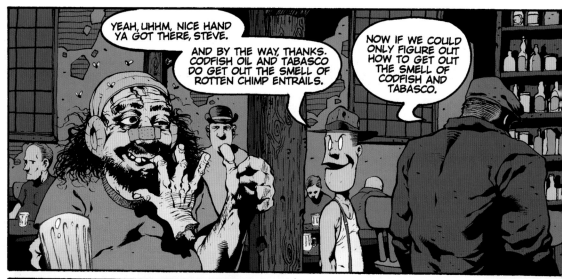

YEAH, UHHM, NICE HAND YA GOT THERE, STEVE.

AND BY THE WAY, THANKS. CODFISH OIL AND TABASCO DO GET OUT THE SMELL OF ROTTEN CHIMP ENTRAILS.

NOW IF WE COULD ONLY FIGURE OUT HOW TO GET OUT THE SMELL OF CODFISH AND TABASCO.

HAYA, NORTON. BURGER ME, WILL YA. YOU KNOW HOW I LIKE EM'.

MIGHT AS WELL MAKE IT TWO.

SURE THING. HAVE A COLD ONE WHILE YA WAIT.

YOU GUYS HEAR WHAT HAPPENED TO BRICK HEAD JOHNNY?

YOU TALKIN' 'BOUT HIM GETTIN' CAUGHT WITH THAT LOBSTER IN HIS PANTS?

OR ARE YA TALKIN' 'BOUT HIM CHUCKIN' THAT OLD LADY AT THAT MONKEY FACE BOY MOMO?

NO, NO, NO, THE ZOMBIES WHACKED HIM YESTERDAY DOWN THE STREET THERE.

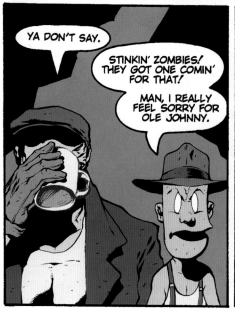

YA DON'T SAY.

STINKIN' ZOMBIES! THEY GOT ONE COMIN' FOR THAT!

MAN, I REALLY FEEL SORRY FOR OLE JOHNNY.

I FEEL SORRY FOR ANYBODY THAT DIED KNOWIN' YOU ON A FIRST NAME BASIS.

I...

YEAH... ME TOO.

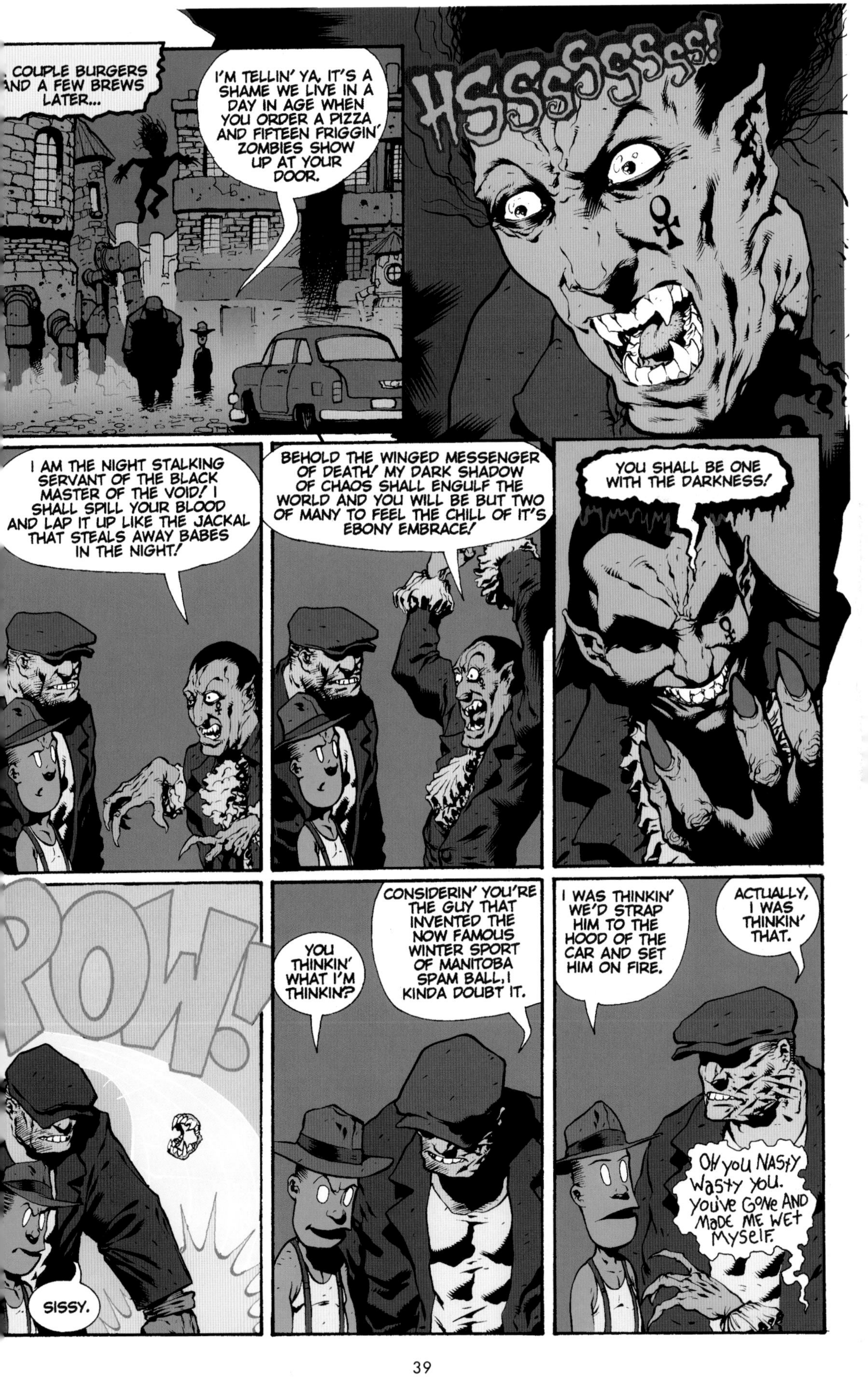
COUPLE BURGERS AND A FEW BREWS LATER...
I'M TELLIN' YA, IT'S A SHAME WE LIVE IN A DAY IN AGE WHEN YOU ORDER A PIZZA AND FIFTEEN FRIGGIN' ZOMBIES SHOW UP AT YOUR DOOR.
HSSSSSSSS!
I AM THE NIGHT STALKING SERVANT OF THE BLACK MASTER OF THE VOID! I SHALL SPILL YOUR BLOOD AND LAP IT UP LIKE THE JACKAL THAT STEALS AWAY BABES IN THE NIGHT!
BEHOLD THE WINGED MESSENGER OF DEATH! MY DARK SHADOW OF CHAOS SHALL ENGULF THE WORLD AND YOU WILL BE BUT TWO OF MANY TO FEEL THE CHILL OF IT'S EBONY EMBRACE!
YOU SHALL BE ONE WITH THE DARKNESS!
POW!
SISSY.
YOU THINKIN' WHAT I'M THINKIN?
CONSIDERIN' YOU'RE THE GUY THAT INVENTED THE NOW FAMOUS WINTER SPORT OF MANITOBA SPAM BALL, I KINDA DOUBT IT.
I WAS THINKIN' WE'D STRAP HIM TO THE HOOD OF THE CAR AND SET HIM ON FIRE.
ACTUALLY, I WAS THINKIN' THAT.
OH YOU NASTY WASTY YOU. YOU'VE GONE AND MADE ME WET MYSELF.

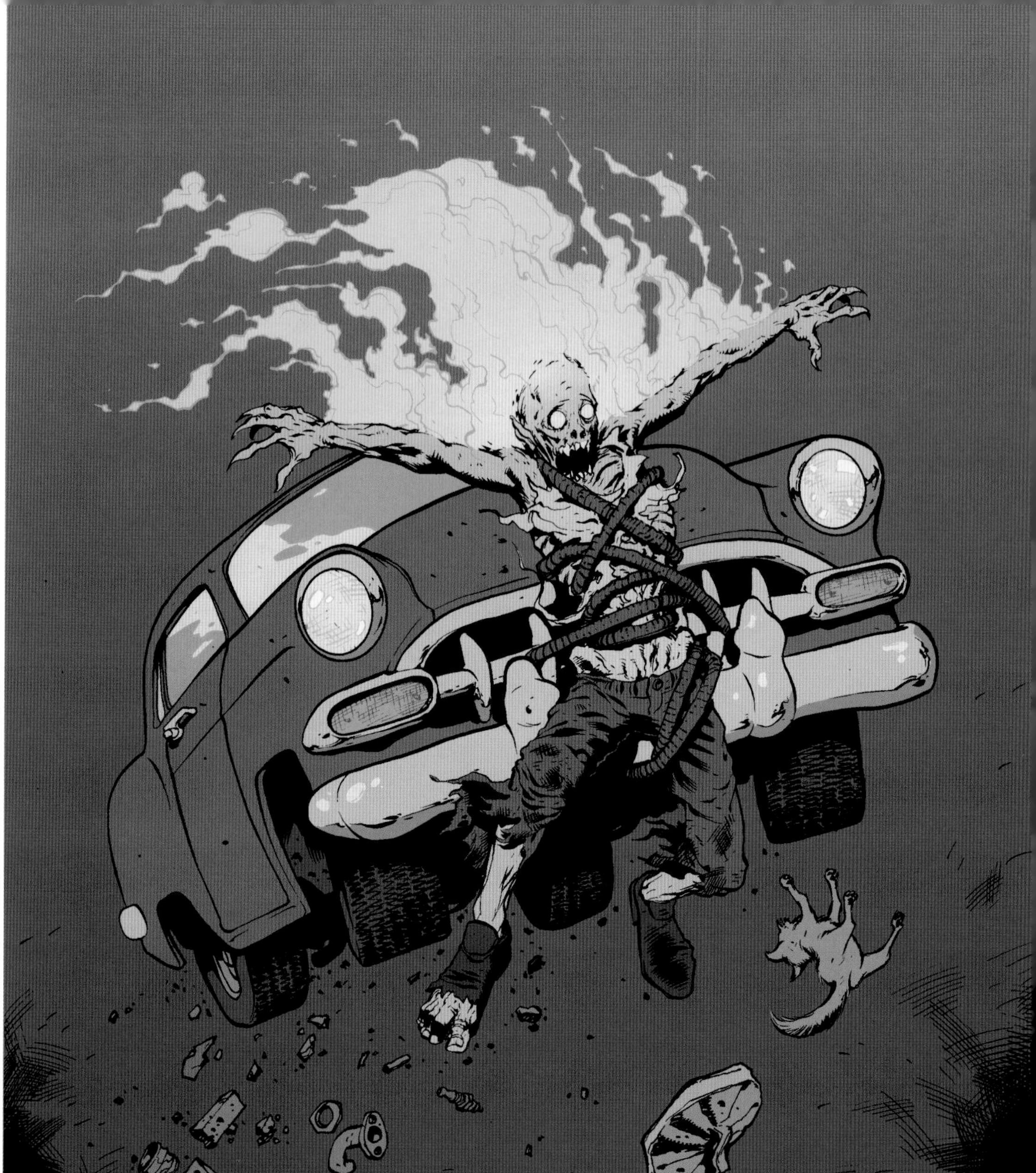

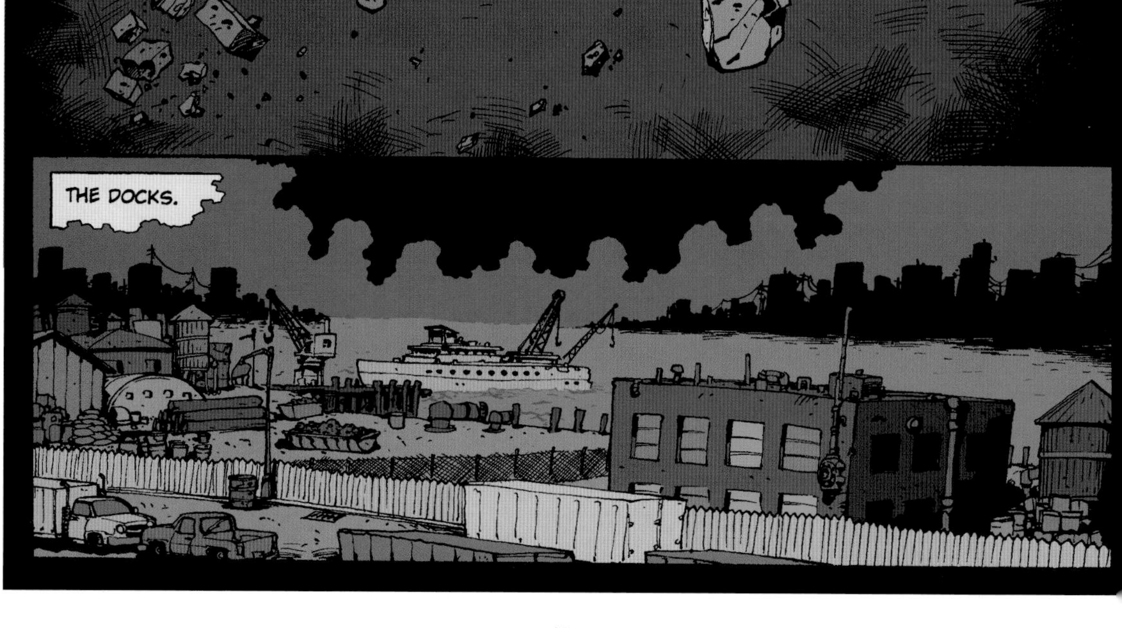
THE DOCKS.

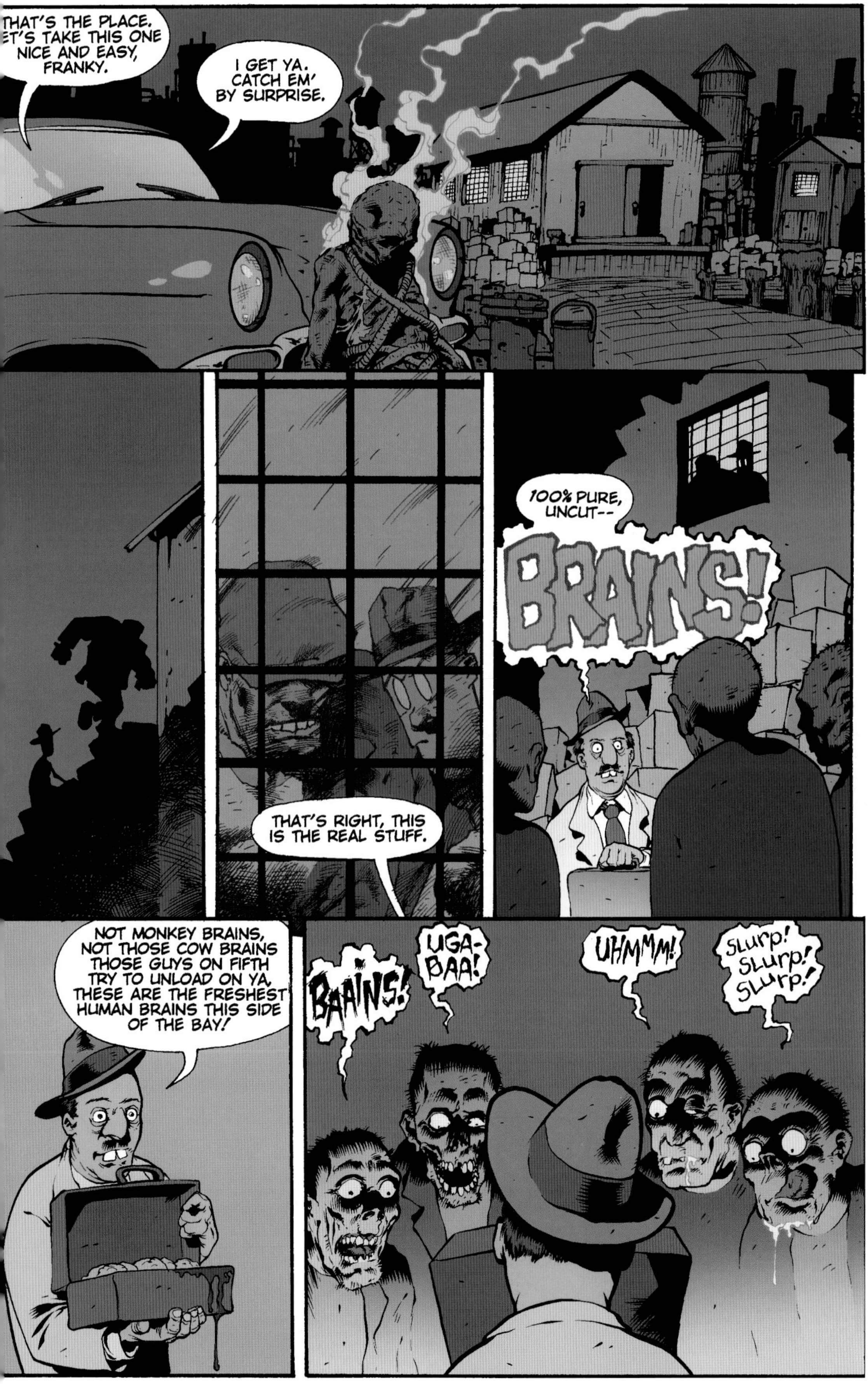

THAT'S THE PLACE. ET'S TAKE THIS ONE NICE AND EASY, FRANKY.
I GET YA. CATCH EM' BY SURPRISE.
100% PURE, UNCUT--
BRAINS!
THAT'S RIGHT, THIS IS THE REAL STUFF.
NOT MONKEY BRAINS, NOT THOSE COW BRAINS THOSE GUYS ON FIFTH TRY TO UNLOAD ON YA. THESE ARE THE FRESHEST HUMAN BRAINS THIS SIDE OF THE BAY!
BRAINS!
UGA-BAA!
UHMMM!
Slurp! Slurp! Slurp!

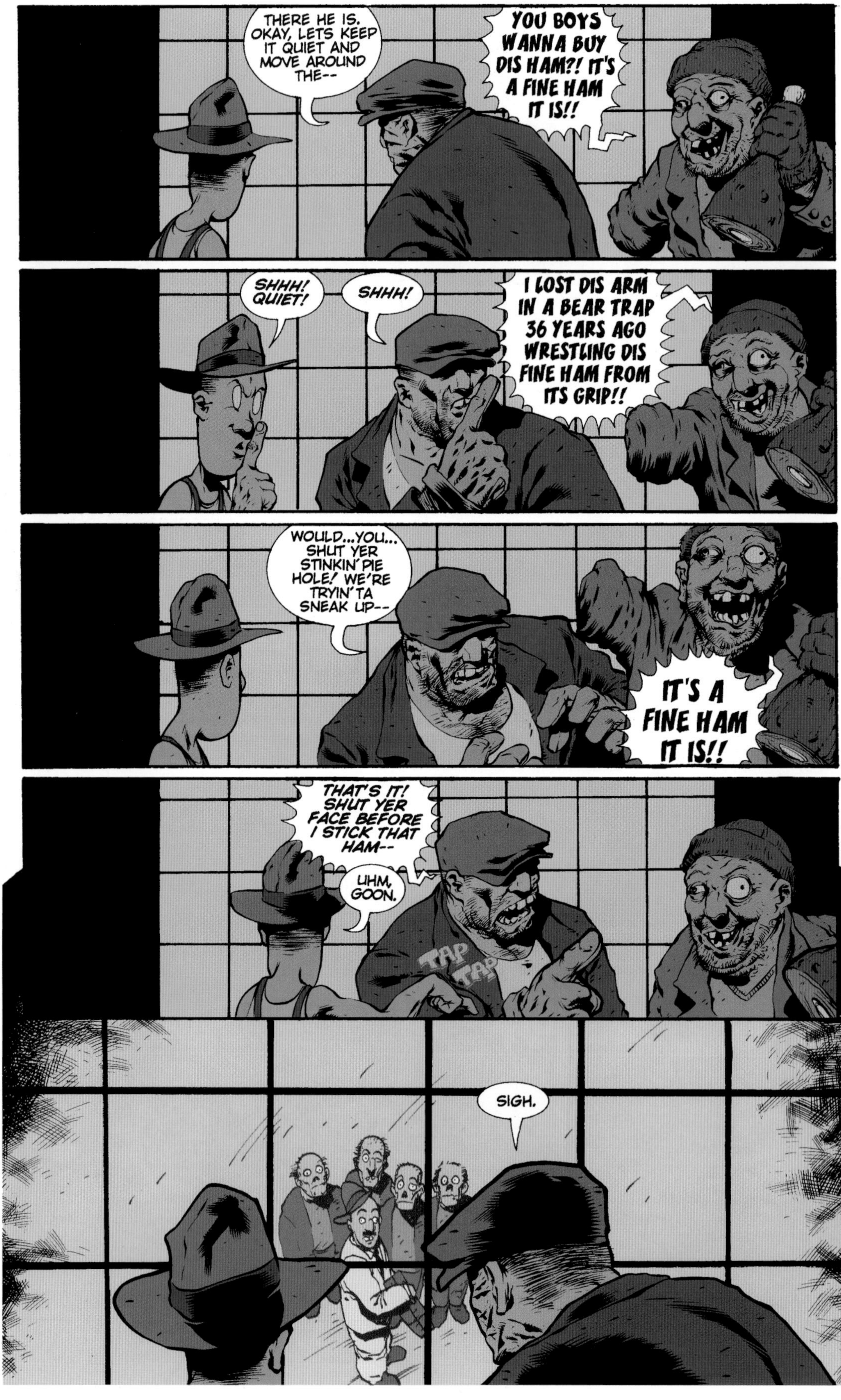
THERE HE IS. OKAY, LETS KEEP IT QUIET AND MOVE AROUND THE--
YOU BOYS WANNA BUY DIS HAM?! IT'S A FINE HAM IT IS!!
SHHH! QUIET!
SHHH!
I LOST DIS ARM IN A BEAR TRAP 36 YEARS AGO WRESTLING DIS FINE HAM FROM ITS GRIP!!
WOULD...YOU... SHUT YER STINKIN' PIE HOLE! WE'RE TRYIN' TA SNEAK UP--
IT'S A FINE HAM IT IS!!
THAT'S IT! SHUT YER FACE BEFORE I STICK THAT HAM--
UHM, GOON.
TAP TAP
SIGH.

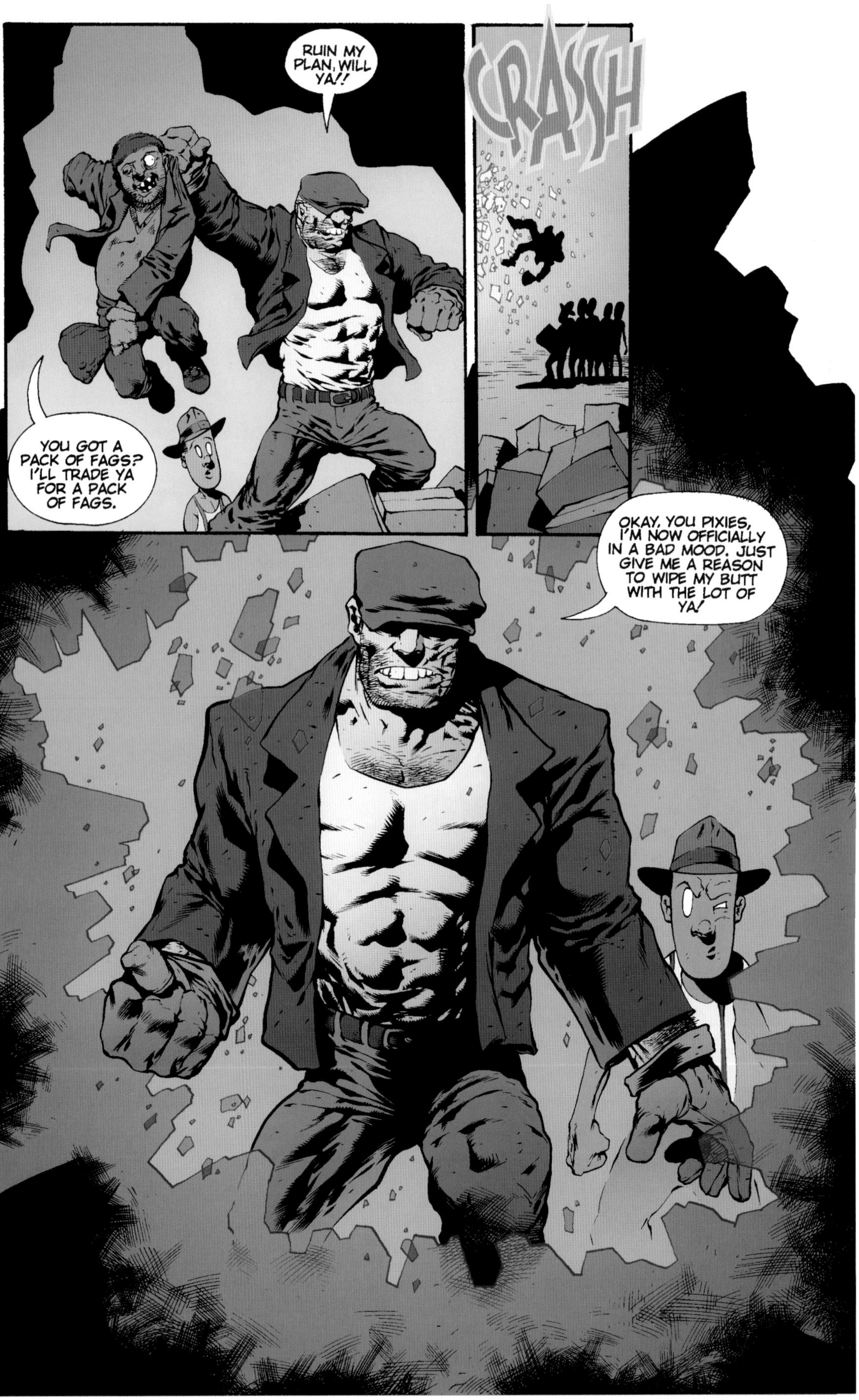
RUIN MY PLAN, WILL YA!!
YOU GOT A PACK OF FAGS? I'LL TRADE YA FOR A PACK OF FAGS.
CRASH
OKAY, YOU PIXIES, I'M NOW OFFICIALLY IN A BAD MOOD. JUST GIVE ME A REASON TO WIPE MY BUTT WITH THE LOT OF YA!

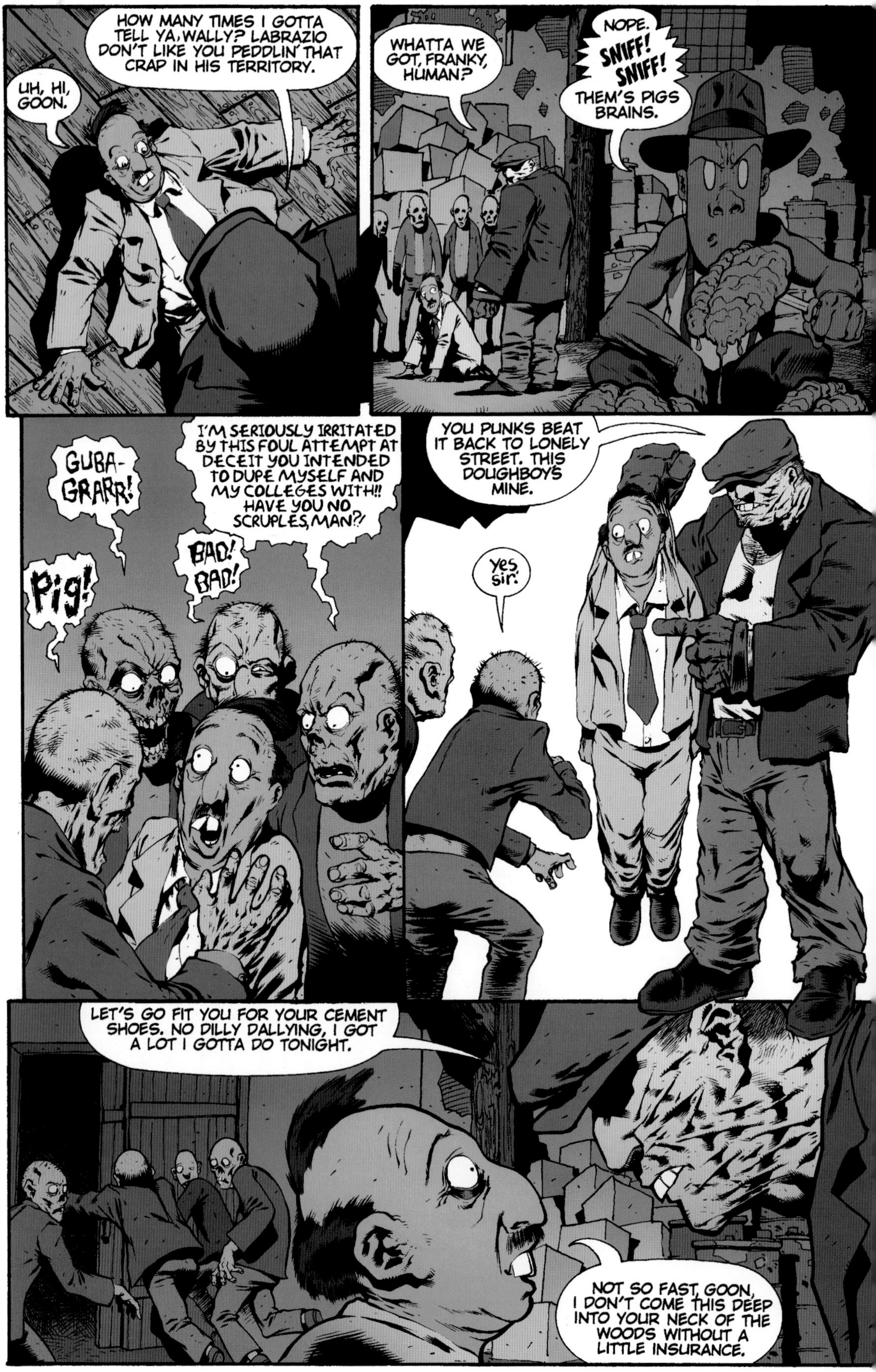
HOW MANY TIMES I GOTTA TELL YA, WALLY? LABRAZIO DON'T LIKE YOU PEDDLIN' THAT CRAP IN HIS TERRITORY.
UH, HI, GOON.
WHATTA WE GOT, FRANKY, HUMAN?
NOPE.
SNIFF! SNIFF!
THEM'S PIGS BRAINS.
GUBA-GRARR!
I'M SERIOUSLY IRRITATED BY THIS FOUL ATTEMPT AT DECEIT YOU INTENDED TO DUPE MYSELF AND MY COLLEGES WITH!! HAVE YOU NO SCRUPLES, MAN?!
BAD! BAD!
PIG!
YOU PUNKS BEAT IT BACK TO LONELY STREET. THIS DOUGHBOY'S MINE.
YES SIR.
LET'S GO FIT YOU FOR YOUR CEMENT SHOES. NO DILLY DALLYING, I GOT A LOT I GOTTA DO TONIGHT.
NOT SO FAST, GOON, I DON'T COME THIS DEEP INTO YOUR NECK OF THE WOODS WITHOUT A LITTLE INSURANCE.

45

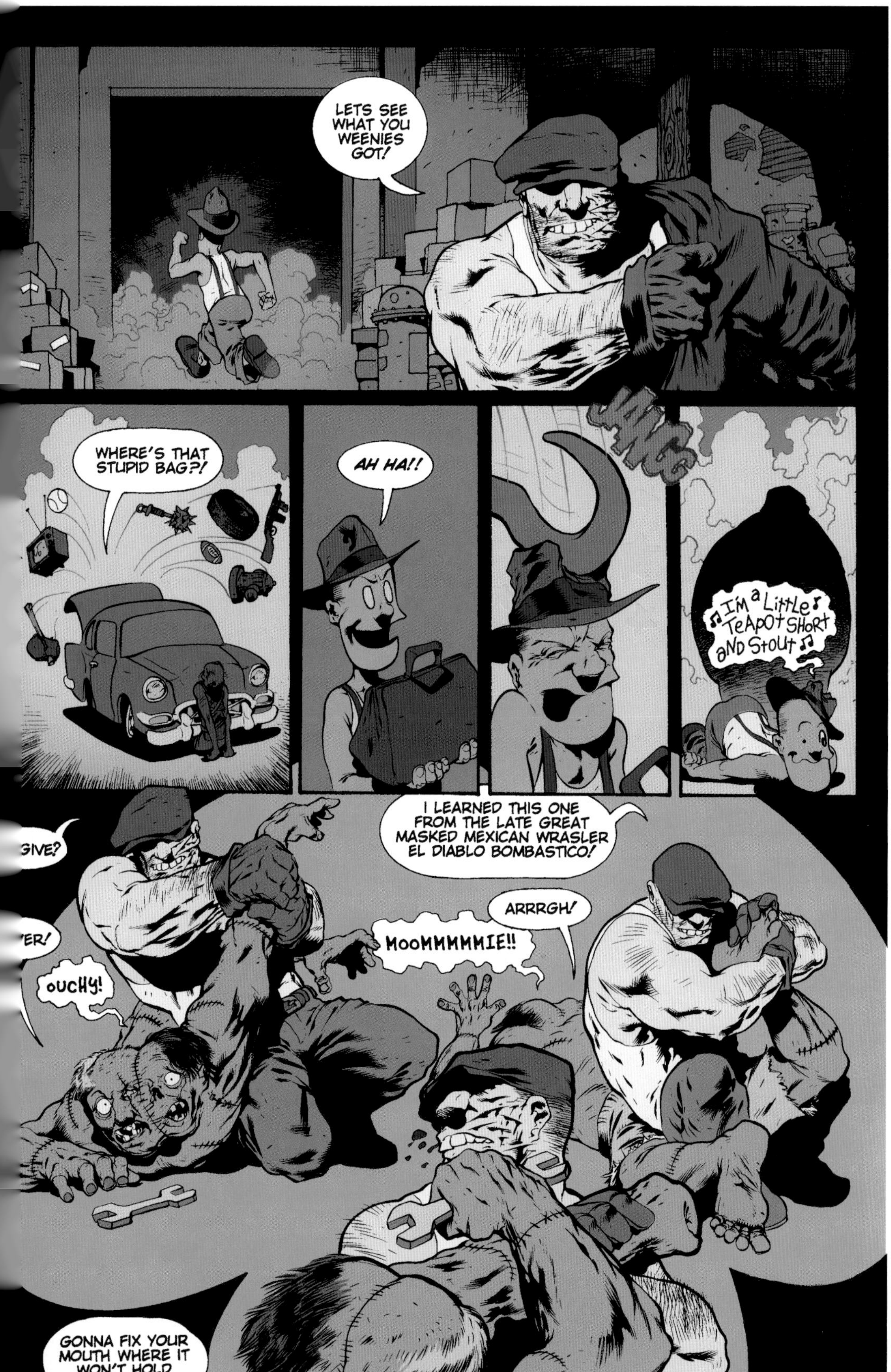
LETS SEE WHAT YOU WEENIES GOT!
WHERE'S THAT STUPID BAG?!
AH HA!!
I'M a Little TeApot Short aND Stout
I LEARNED THIS ONE FROM THE LATE GREAT MASKED MEXICAN WRASLER EL DIABLO BOMBASTICO!
GIVE?
ER!
OUCHY!
ARRRGH!
MOOMMMMMIE!!
GONNA FIX YOUR MOUTH WHERE IT WON'T HOLD SOUP, GOON!

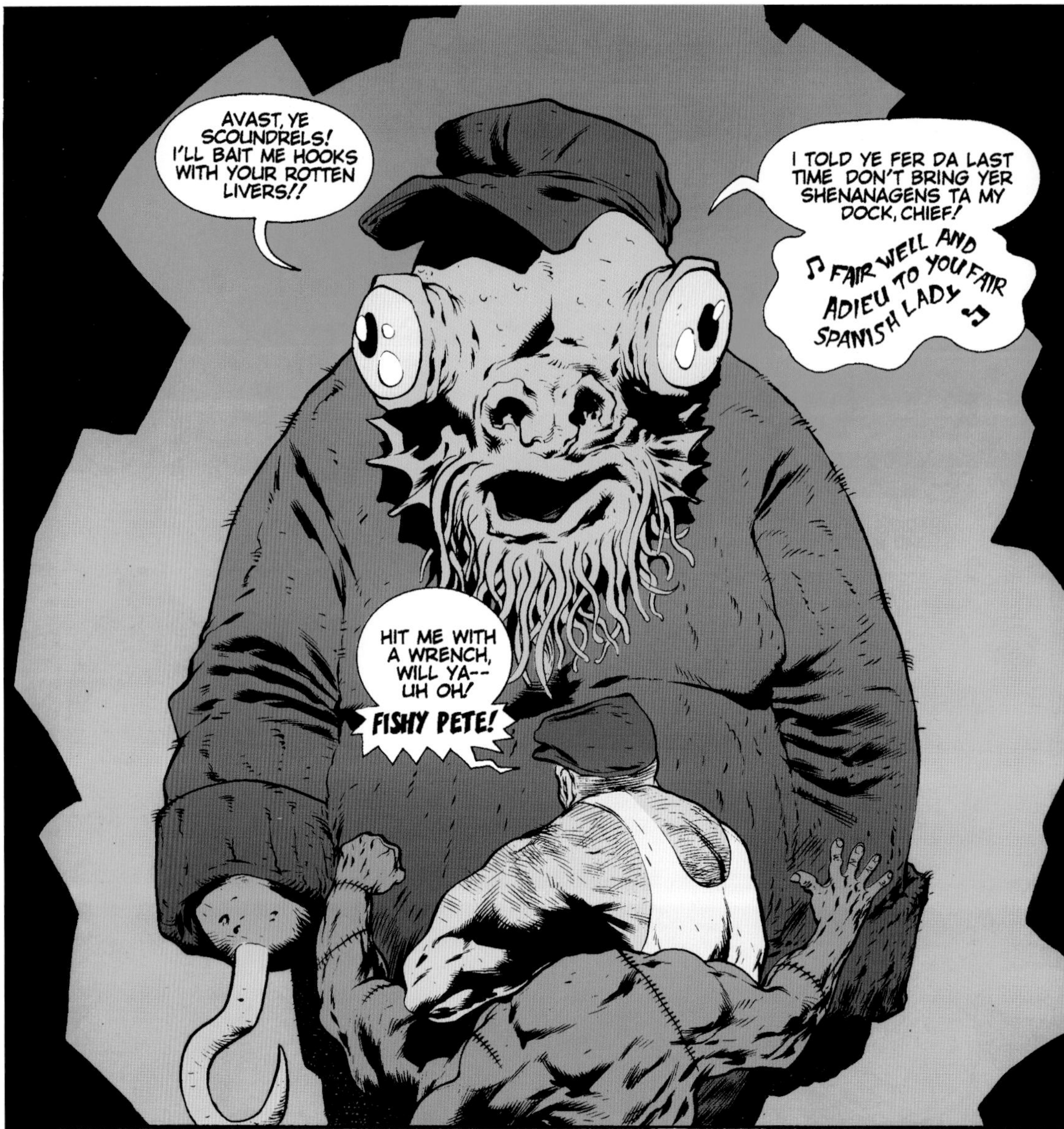
AVAST, YE SCOUNDRELS! I'LL BAIT ME HOOKS WITH YOUR ROTTEN LIVERS!!
I TOLD YE FER DA LAST TIME DON'T BRING YER SHENANAGENS TA MY DOCK, CHIEF!
♫ FAIR WELL AND ADIEU TO YOU FAIR SPANISH LADY ♫
HIT ME WITH A WRENCH, WILL YA-- UH OH!
FISHY PETE!

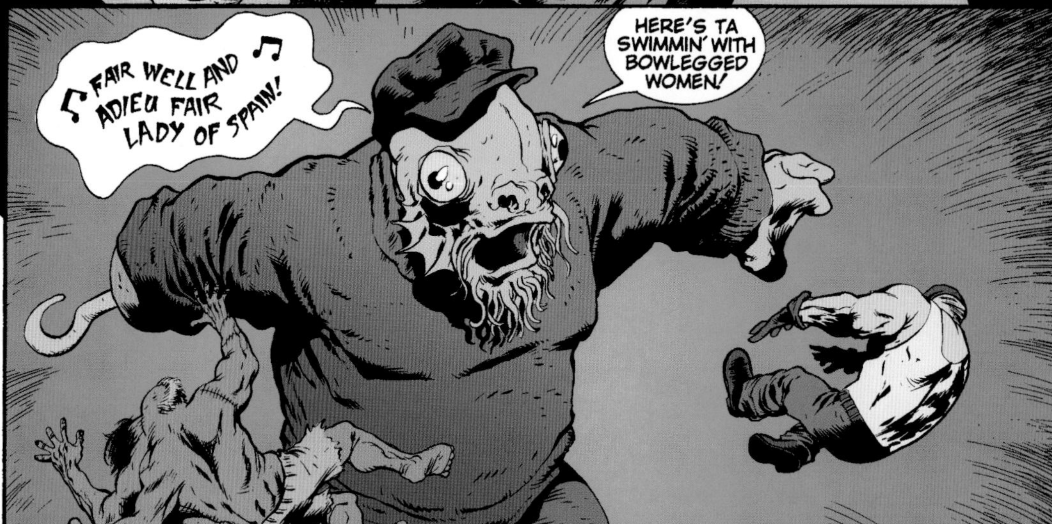
♫ FAIR WELL AND ADIEU FAIR LADY OF SPAIN! ♫
HERE'S TA SWIMMIN' WITH BOWLEGGED WOMEN!

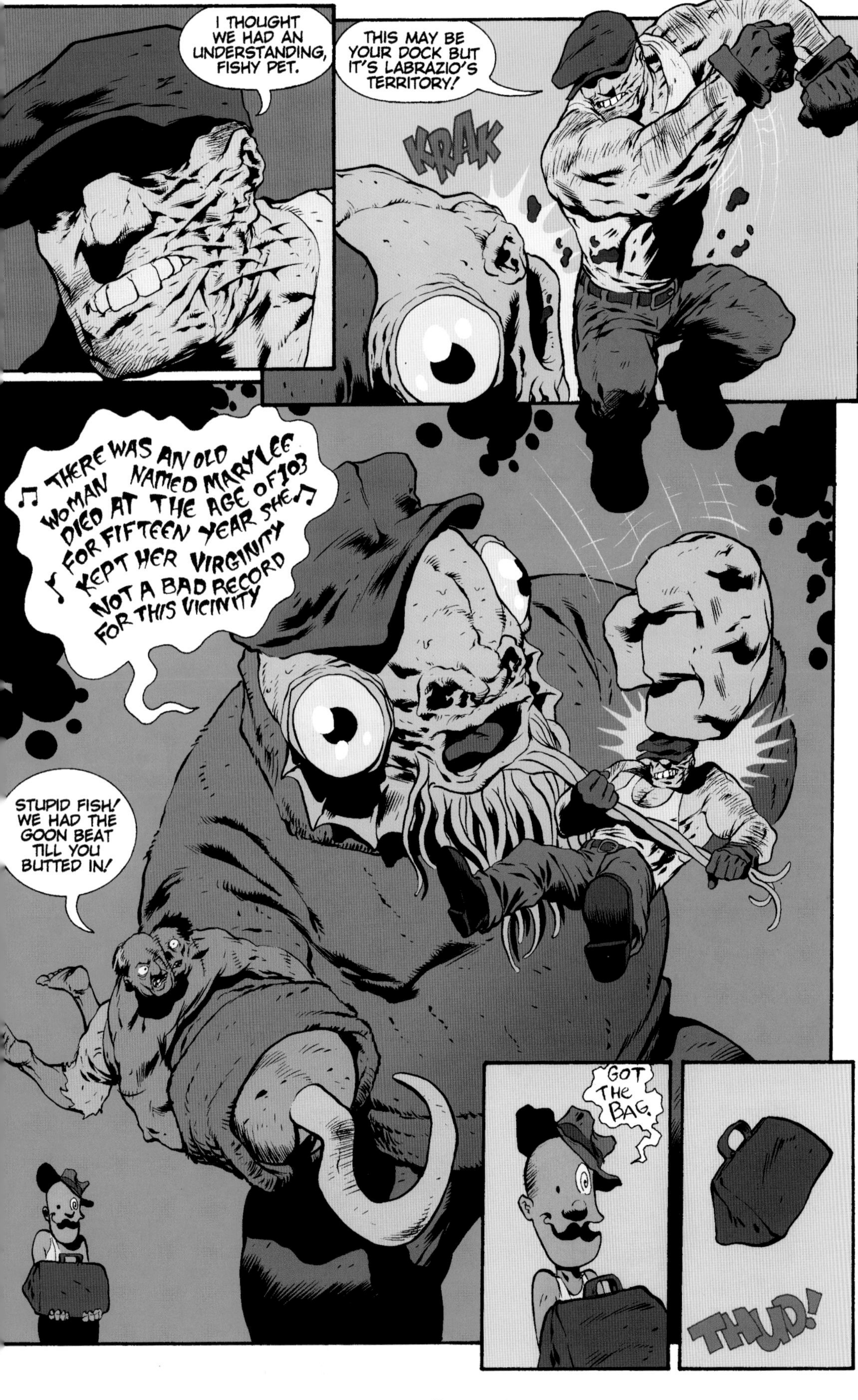

I THOUGHT WE HAD AN UNDERSTANDING, FISHY PET.
THIS MAY BE YOUR DOCK BUT IT'S LABRAZIO'S TERRITORY!
KRAK
♫ THERE WAS AN OLD WOMAN NAMED MARYLEE DIED AT THE AGE OF 103 FOR FIFTEEN YEAR SHE ♫ KEPT HER VIRGINITY NOT A BAD RECORD FOR THIS VICINITY
STUPID FISH! WE HAD THE GOON BEAT TILL YOU BUTTED IN!
GOT THE BAG.
THUD!

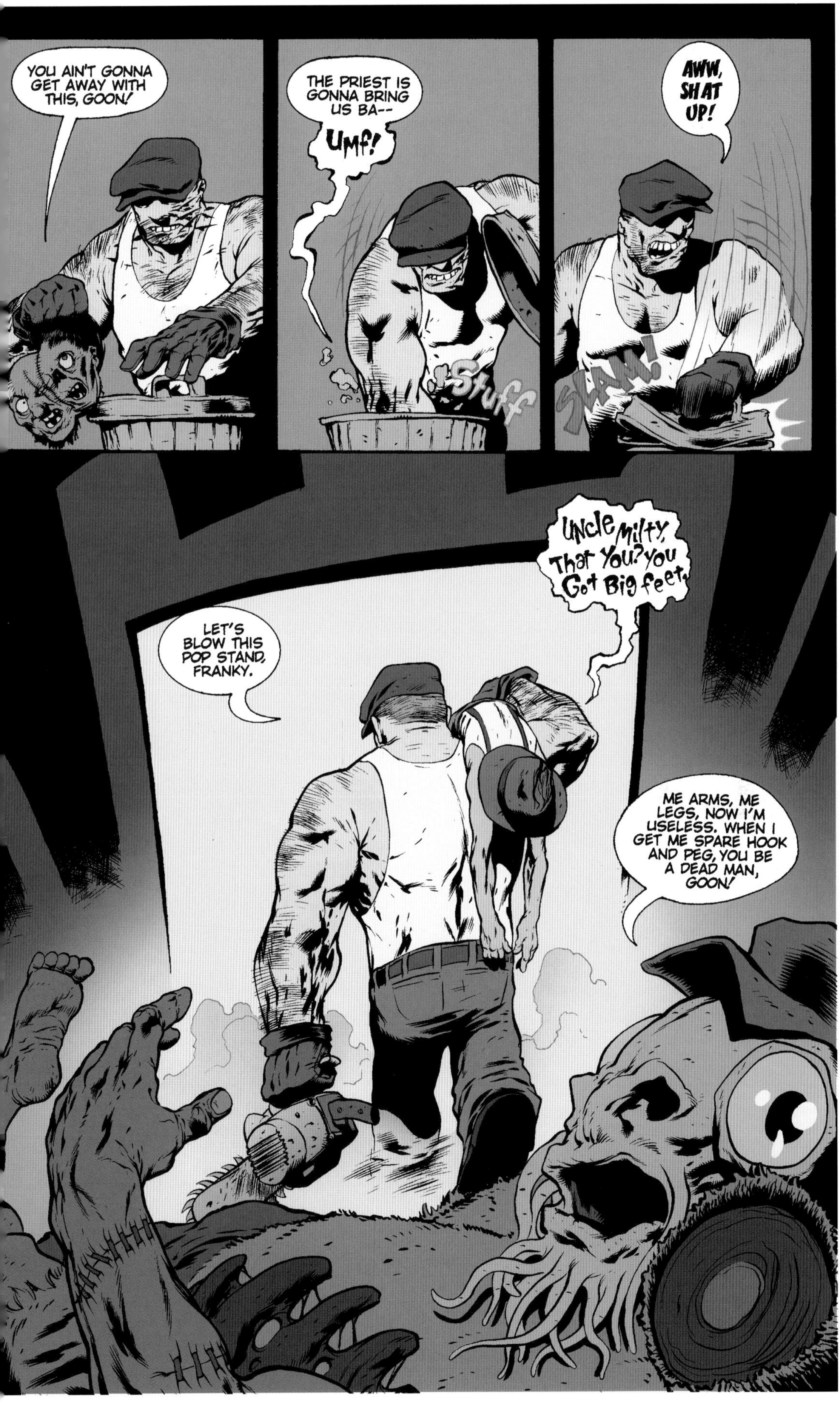
YOU AIN'T GONNA GET AWAY WITH THIS, GOON!
THE PRIEST IS GONNA BRING US BA--
UMF!
STUFF
AWW, SHAT UP!
SLAM!
UNCLE MILTY, THAT YOU? YOU GOT BIG FEET.
LET'S BLOW THIS POP STAND, FRANKY.
ME ARMS, ME LEGS, NOW I'M USELESS. WHEN I GET ME SPARE HOOK AND PEG, YOU BE A DEAD MAN, GOON!

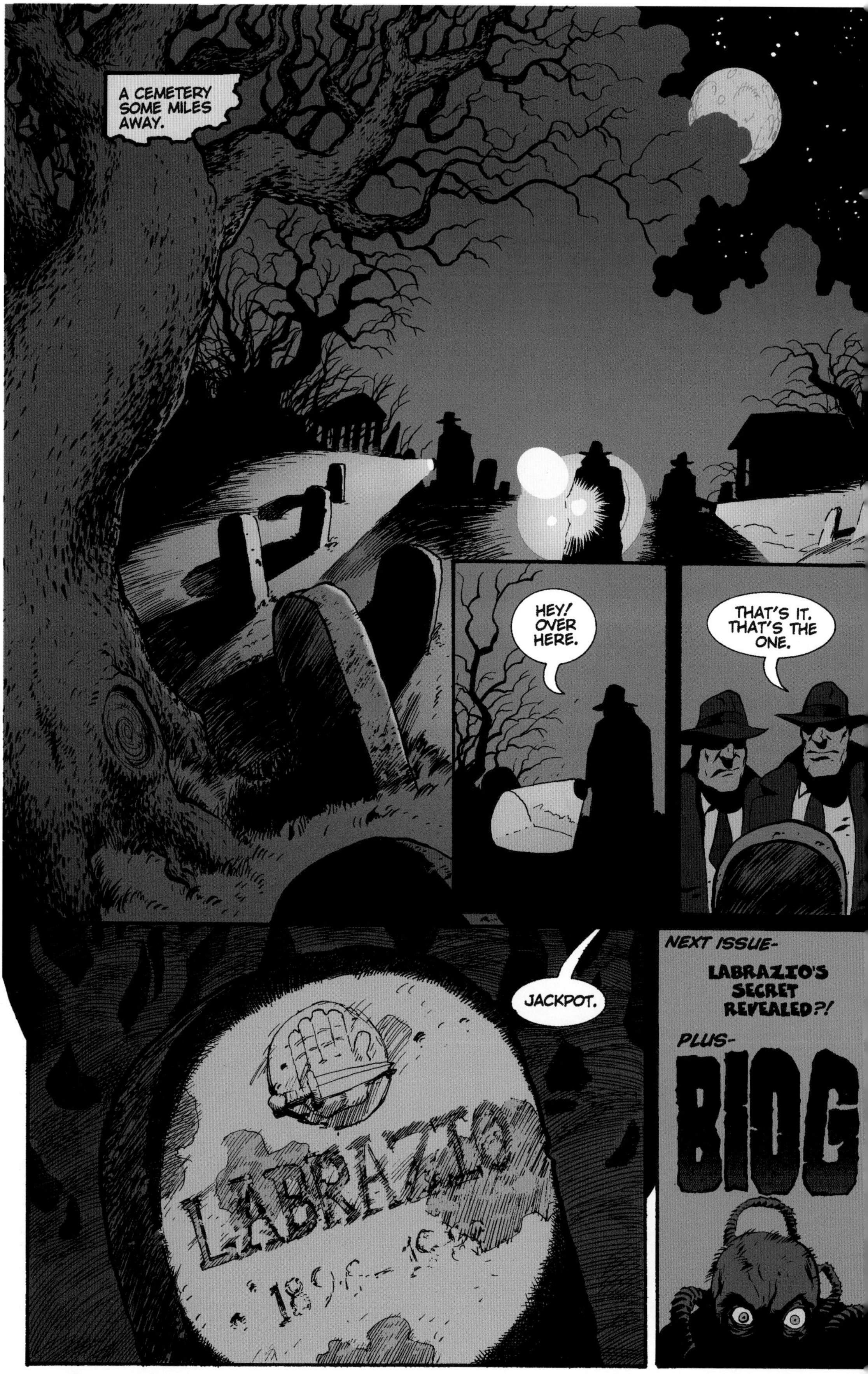
A CEMETERY SOME MILES AWAY.
HEY! OVER HERE.
THAT'S IT. THAT'S THE ONE.
JACKPOT.
LABRAZIO
NEXT ISSUE-
LABRAZIO'S SECRET REVEALED?!
PLUS-
BIOG

# CHAPTER 3

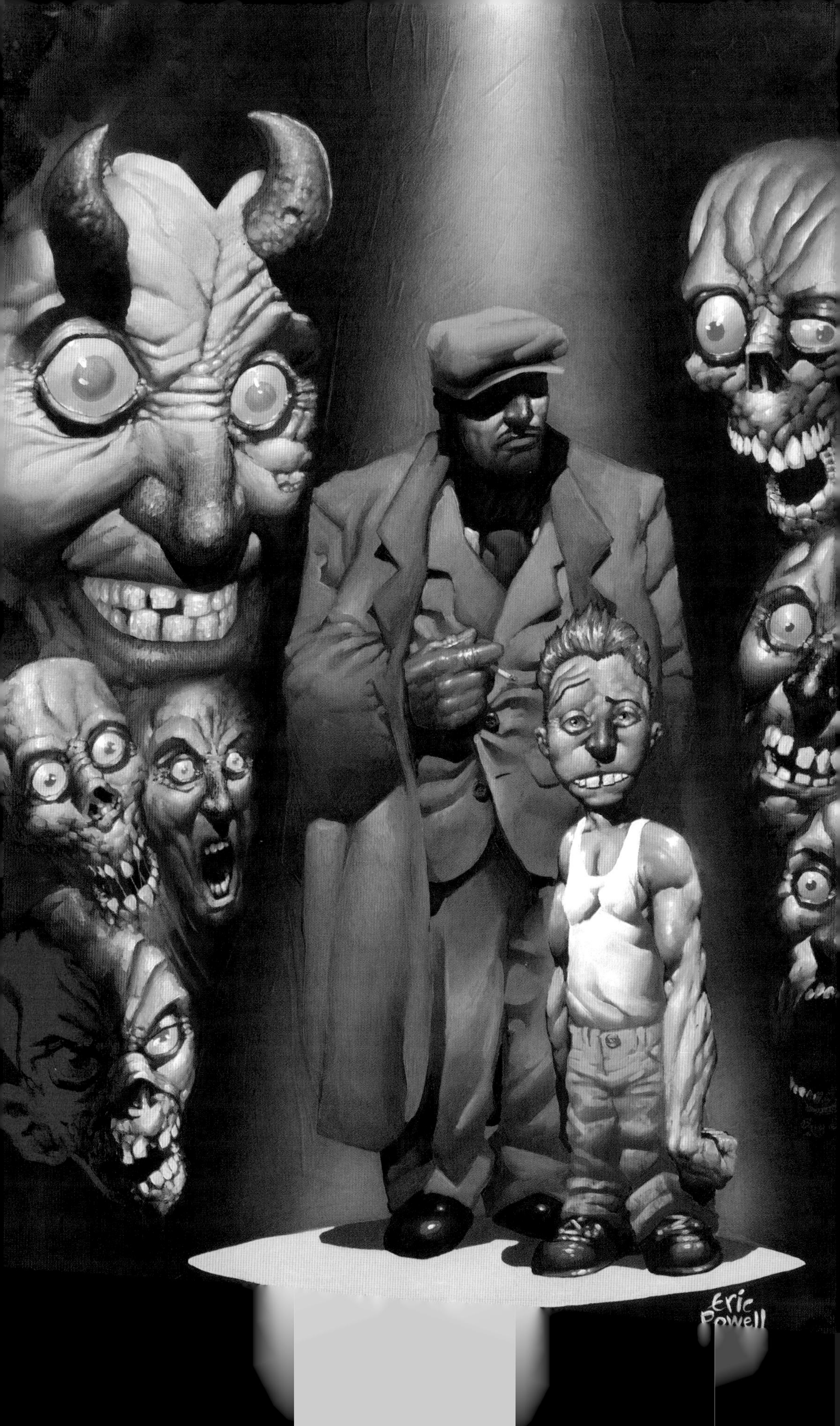
Eric Powell

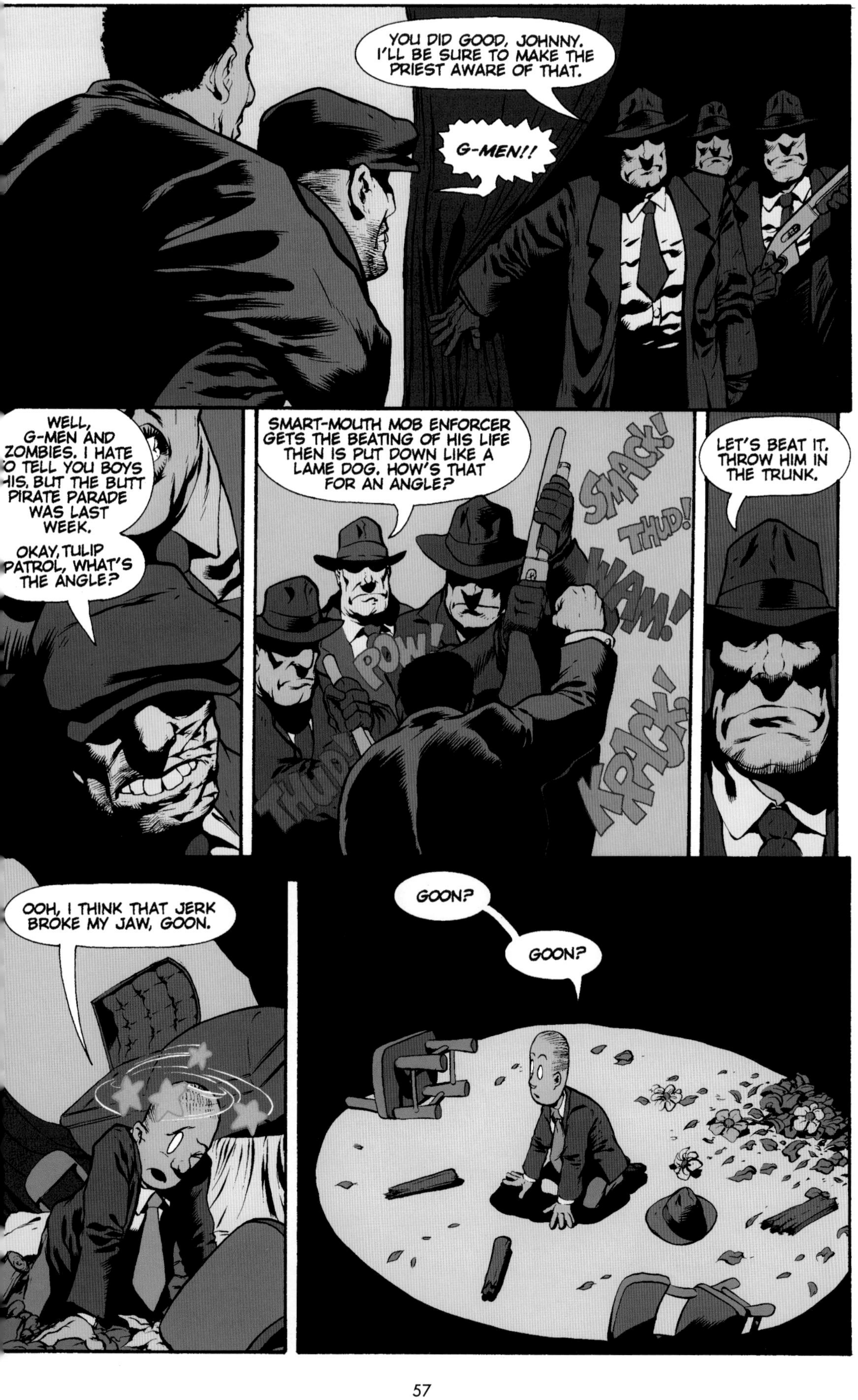
YOU DID GOOD, JOHNNY. I'LL BE SURE TO MAKE THE PRIEST AWARE OF THAT.
G-MEN!!
WELL, G-MEN AND ZOMBIES. I HATE TO TELL YOU BOYS THIS, BUT THE BUTT PIRATE PARADE WAS LAST WEEK.
OKAY, TULIP PATROL, WHAT'S THE ANGLE?
SMART-MOUTH MOB ENFORCER GETS THE BEATING OF HIS LIFE THEN IS PUT DOWN LIKE A LAME DOG. HOW'S THAT FOR AN ANGLE?
SMACK!
THUD!
WAM!
POW!
THUD!
KRACK!
LET'S BEAT IT. THROW HIM IN THE TRUNK.
OOH, I THINK THAT JERK BROKE MY JAW, GOON.
GOON?
GOON?

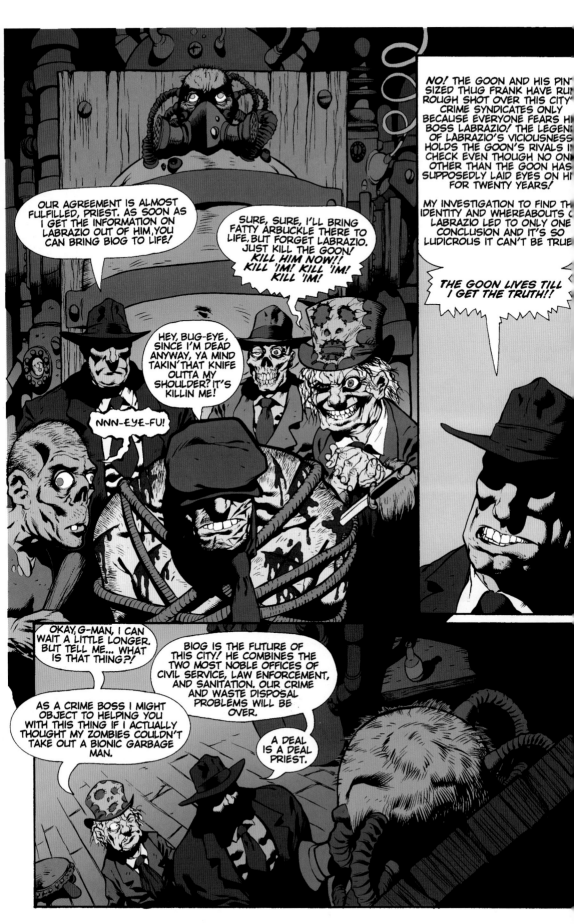

OUR AGREEMENT IS ALMOST FULFILLED, PRIEST. AS SOON AS I GET THE INFORMATION ON LABRAZIO OUT OF HIM, YOU CAN BRING BIOG TO LIFE!

SURE, SURE, I'LL BRING FATTY ARBUCKLE THERE TO LIFE, BUT FORGET LABRAZIO. JUST KILL THE GOON! *KILL HIM NOW!! KILL 'IM! KILL 'IM! KILL 'IM!*

*NO!* THE GOON AND HIS PIN SIZED THUG FRANK HAVE RU ROUGH SHOT OVER THIS CITY CRIME SYNDICATES ONLY BECAUSE EVERYONE FEARS H BOSS LABRAZIO! THE LEGEN OF LABRAZIO'S VICIOUSNESS HOLDS THE GOON'S RIVALS I CHECK EVEN THOUGH NO ON OTHER THAN THE GOON HAS SUPPOSEDLY LAID EYES ON HI FOR TWENTY YEARS!

MY INVESTIGATION TO FIND T IDENTITY AND WHEREABOUTS LABRAZIO LED TO ONLY ONE CONCLUSION AND IT'S SO LUDICROUS IT CAN'T BE TRUE

*THE GOON LIVES TILL I GET THE TRUTH!!*

HEY, BUG-EYE, SINCE I'M DEAD ANYWAY, YA MIND TAKIN' THAT KNIFE OUTTA MY SHOULDER? IT'S KILLIN ME!

NNN-EYE-FU!

OKAY, G-MAN, I CAN WAIT A LITTLE LONGER. BUT TELL ME... WHAT IS THAT THING?!

BIOG IS THE FUTURE OF THIS CITY! HE COMBINES THE TWO MOST NOBLE OFFICES OF CIVIL SERVICE, LAW ENFORCEMENT, AND SANITATION. OUR CRIME AND WASTE DISPOSAL PROBLEMS WILL BE OVER.

AS A CRIME BOSS I MIGHT OBJECT TO HELPING YOU WITH THIS THING IF I ACTUALLY THOUGHT MY ZOMBIES COULDN'T TAKE OUT A BIONIC GARBAGE MAN.

A DEAL IS A DEAL PRIEST.

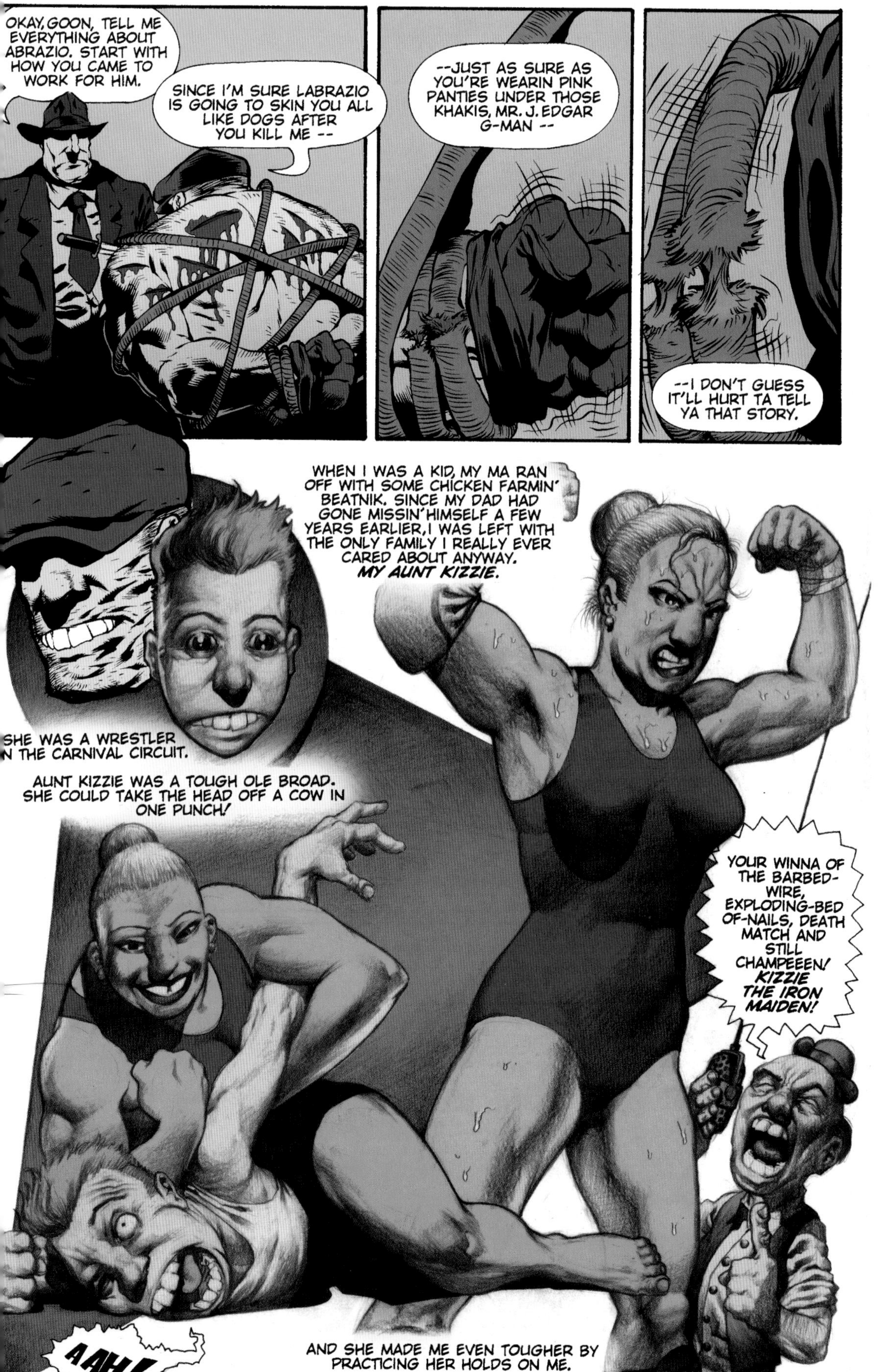
OKAY, GOON, TELL ME EVERYTHING ABOUT ABRAZIO. START WITH HOW YOU CAME TO WORK FOR HIM.
SINCE I'M SURE LABRAZIO IS GOING TO SKIN YOU ALL LIKE DOGS AFTER YOU KILL ME --
--JUST AS SURE AS YOU'RE WEARIN PINK PANTIES UNDER THOSE KHAKIS, MR. J. EDGAR G-MAN --
--I DON'T GUESS IT'LL HURT TA TELL YA THAT STORY.
WHEN I WAS A KID, MY MA RAN OFF WITH SOME CHICKEN FARMIN' BEATNIK. SINCE MY DAD HAD GONE MISSIN' HIMSELF A FEW YEARS EARLIER, I WAS LEFT WITH THE ONLY FAMILY I REALLY EVER CARED ABOUT ANYWAY. MY AUNT KIZZIE.
SHE WAS A WRESTLER N THE CARNIVAL CIRCUIT.
AUNT KIZZIE WAS A TOUGH OLE BROAD. SHE COULD TAKE THE HEAD OFF A COW IN ONE PUNCH!
YOUR WINNA OF THE BARBED-WIRE, EXPLODING-BED OF-NAILS, DEATH MATCH AND STILL CHAMPEEEN! KIZZIE THE IRON MAIDEN!
AAH!
AND SHE MADE ME EVEN TOUGHER BY PRACTICING HER HOLDS ON ME.

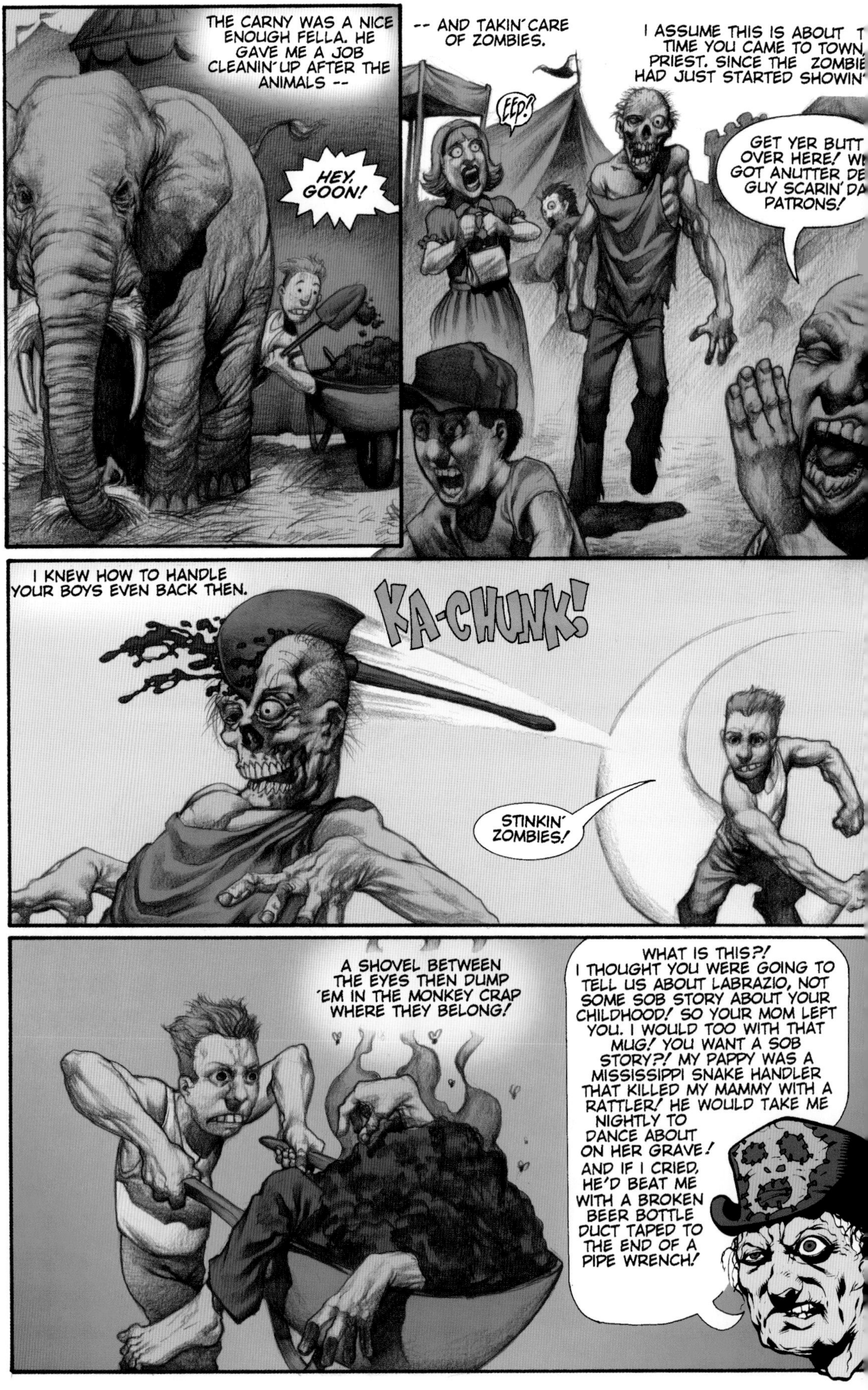

THE CARNY WAS A NICE ENOUGH FELLA. HE GAVE ME A JOB CLEANIN' UP AFTER THE ANIMALS --
HEY, GOON!
-- AND TAKIN' CARE OF ZOMBIES.
I ASSUME THIS IS ABOUT T TIME YOU CAME TO TOWN, PRIEST. SINCE THE ZOMBIE HAD JUST STARTED SHOWIN'
EEP?!
GET YER BUTT OVER HERE! W GOT ANUTTER DE GUY SCARIN' DA PATRONS!
I KNEW HOW TO HANDLE YOUR BOYS EVEN BACK THEN.
KA-CHUNK!
STINKIN' ZOMBIES!
A SHOVEL BETWEEN THE EYES THEN DUMP 'EM IN THE MONKEY CRAP WHERE THEY BELONG!
WHAT IS THIS?! I THOUGHT YOU WERE GOING TO TELL US ABOUT LABRAZIO, NOT SOME SOB STORY ABOUT YOUR CHILDHOOD! SO YOUR MOM LEFT YOU. I WOULD TOO WITH THAT MUG! YOU WANT A SOB STORY?! MY PAPPY WAS A MISSISSIPPI SNAKE HANDLER THAT KILLED MY MAMMY WITH A RATTLER! HE WOULD TAKE ME NIGHTLY TO DANCE ABOUT ON HER GRAVE! AND IF I CRIED, HE'D BEAT ME WITH A BROKEN BEER BOTTLE DUCT TAPED TO THE END OF A PIPE WRENCH!

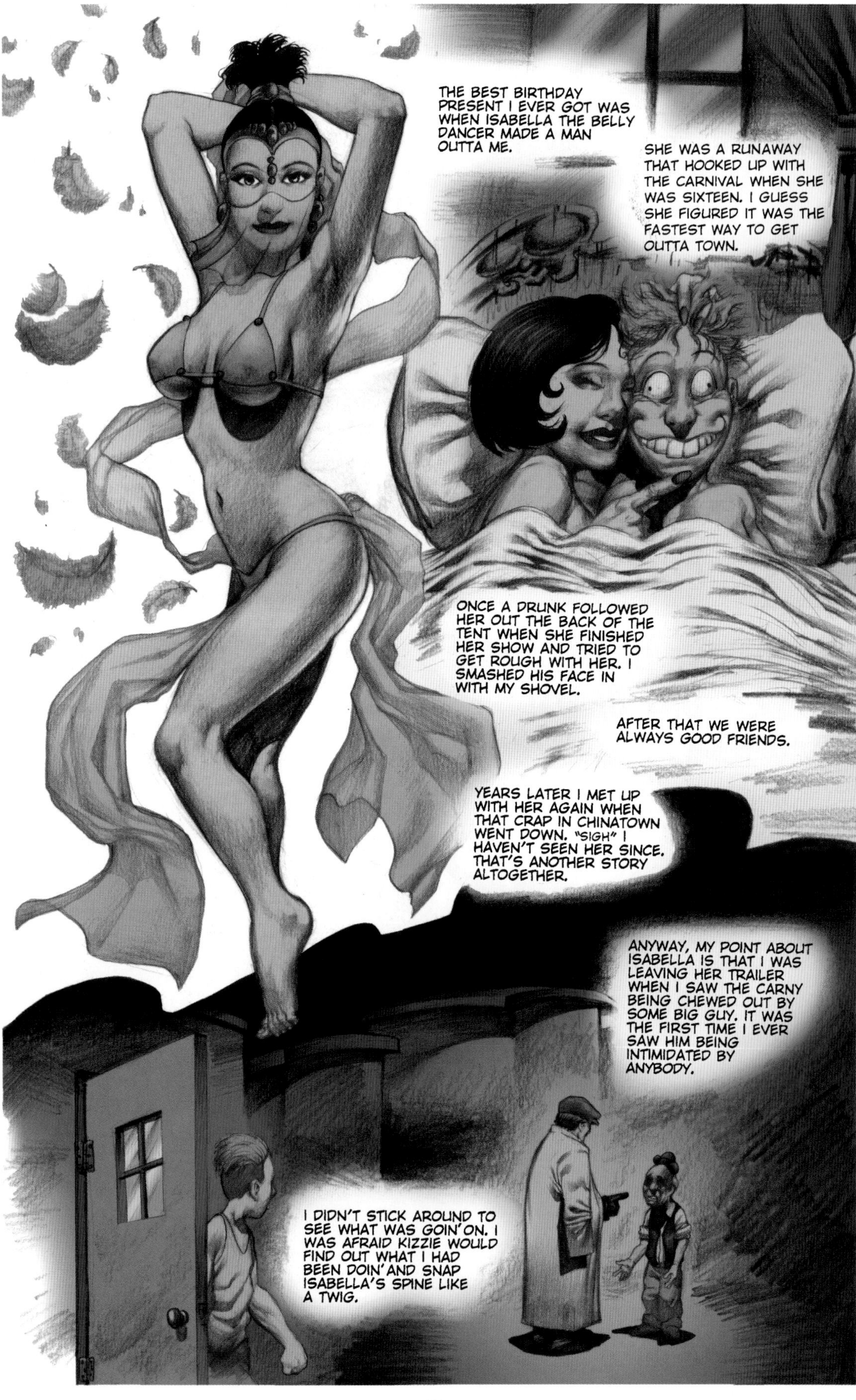
THE BEST BIRTHDAY PRESENT I EVER GOT WAS WHEN ISABELLA THE BELLY DANCER MADE A MAN OUTTA ME.
SHE WAS A RUNAWAY THAT HOOKED UP WITH THE CARNIVAL WHEN SHE WAS SIXTEEN. I GUESS SHE FIGURED IT WAS THE FASTEST WAY TO GET OUTTA TOWN.
ONCE A DRUNK FOLLOWED HER OUT THE BACK OF THE TENT WHEN SHE FINISHED HER SHOW AND TRIED TO GET ROUGH WITH HER. I SMASHED HIS FACE IN WITH MY SHOVEL.
AFTER THAT WE WERE ALWAYS GOOD FRIENDS.
YEARS LATER I MET UP WITH HER AGAIN WHEN THAT CRAP IN CHINATOWN WENT DOWN. "SIGH" I HAVEN'T SEEN HER SINCE. THAT'S ANOTHER STORY ALTOGETHER.
ANYWAY, MY POINT ABOUT ISABELLA IS THAT I WAS LEAVING HER TRAILER WHEN I SAW THE CARNY BEING CHEWED OUT BY SOME BIG GUY. IT WAS THE FIRST TIME I EVER SAW HIM BEING INTIMIDATED BY ANYBODY.
I DIDN'T STICK AROUND TO SEE WHAT WAS GOIN'ON. I WAS AFRAID KIZZIE WOULD FIND OUT WHAT I HAD BEEN DOIN'AND SNAP ISABELLA'S SPINE LIKE A TWIG.

THE NEXT MORNING EVERYONE WAS TALKIN' ABOUT SOME REAL BAD APPLE CALLED LABRAZIO.

APPARENTLY THE CARNY OWED THIS GUY A FAVOR, SO HE HAD TO HIDE HIM WHILE THE COPS WAS LOOKIN' FOR HIM.

EVERYBODY HAD A STORY.

CHEW ON THIS YA FILTHY BRATS!

I HEARD HE LOST A BRIEFCASE FULL OF MONEY, AND SOME OLD GRANDMOTHER FOUND IT. SHE WAS A NICE OLD BROAD SO SHE DONATES IT TO CHARITY. WHEN LABRAZIO FOUND OUT, HE STUFFED THE OLD LADY IN A FIVE GALLON BUCKET AND MAILED IT TO FEED THE CHILDREN!

LOOK AT WHAT HE'S DOING TO THAT DOG!!

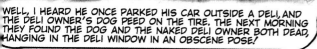

WELL, I HEARD HE ONCE PARKED HIS CAR OUTSIDE A DELI, AND THE DELI OWNER'S DOG PEED ON THE TIRE. THE NEXT MORNING THEY FOUND THE DOG AND THE NAKED DELI OWNER BOTH DEAD, HANGING IN THE DELI WINDOW IN AN OBSCENE POSE!

I HAD TO MEET THIS GUY!!

64

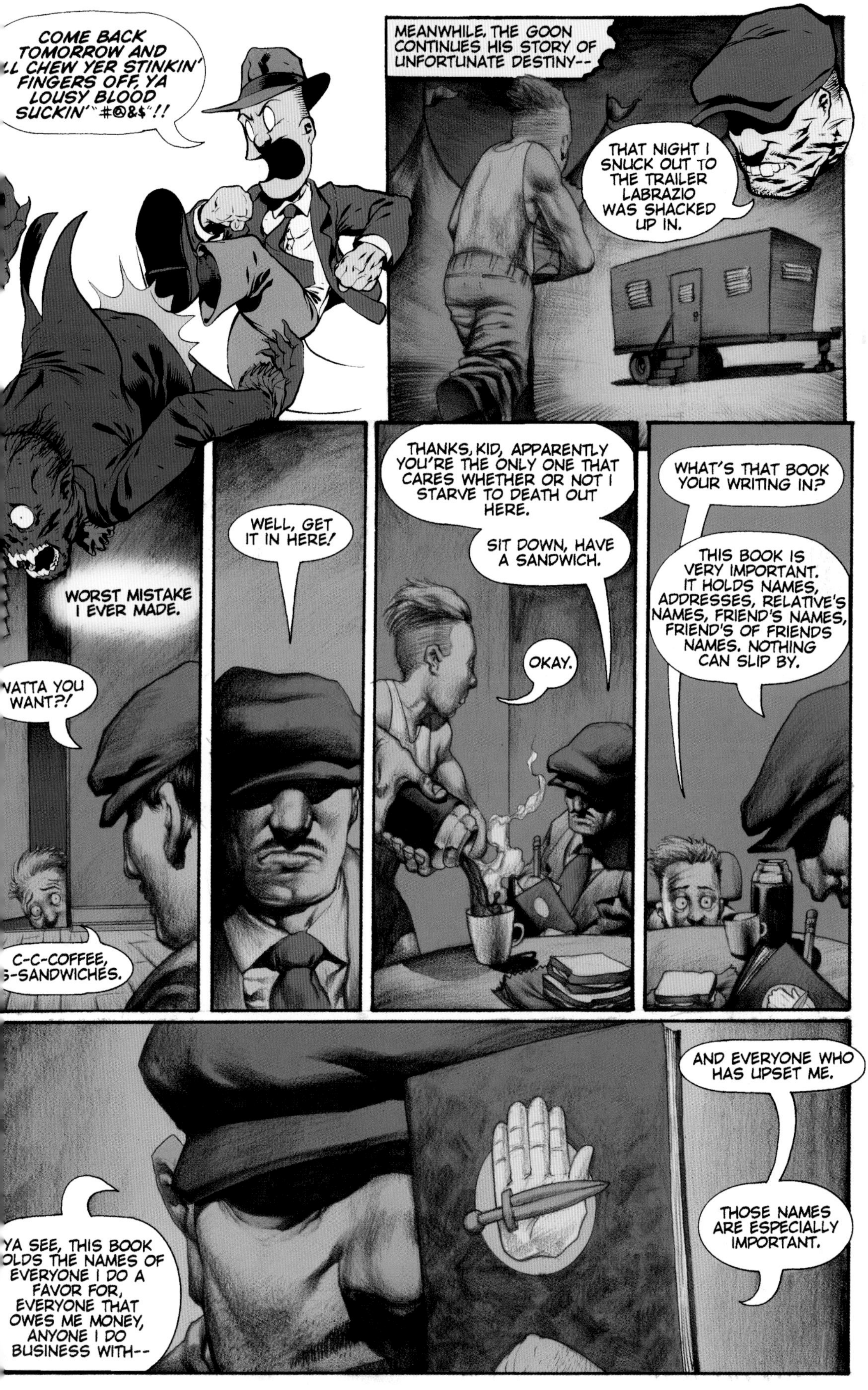
COME BACK TOMORROW AND 'LL CHEW YER STINKIN' FINGERS OFF, YA LOUSY BLOOD SUCKIN' "#®&$"!!
MEANWHILE, THE GOON CONTINUES HIS STORY OF UNFORTUNATE DESTINY--
THAT NIGHT I SNUCK OUT TO THE TRAILER LABRAZIO WAS SHACKED UP IN.
WORST MISTAKE I EVER MADE.
WATTA YOU WANT?!
C-C-COFFEE, S-SANDWICHES.
WELL, GET IT IN HERE!
THANKS, KID, APPARENTLY YOU'RE THE ONLY ONE THAT CARES WHETHER OR NOT I STARVE TO DEATH OUT HERE.
SIT DOWN, HAVE A SANDWICH.
OKAY.
WHAT'S THAT BOOK YOUR WRITING IN?
THIS BOOK IS VERY IMPORTANT. IT HOLDS NAMES, ADDRESSES, RELATIVE'S NAMES, FRIEND'S NAMES, FRIEND'S OF FRIENDS NAMES. NOTHING CAN SLIP BY.
YA SEE, THIS BOOK OLDS THE NAMES OF EVERYONE I DO A FAVOR FOR, EVERYONE THAT OWES ME MONEY, ANYONE I DO BUSINESS WITH--
AND EVERYONE WHO HAS UPSET ME.
THOSE NAMES ARE ESPECIALLY IMPORTANT.

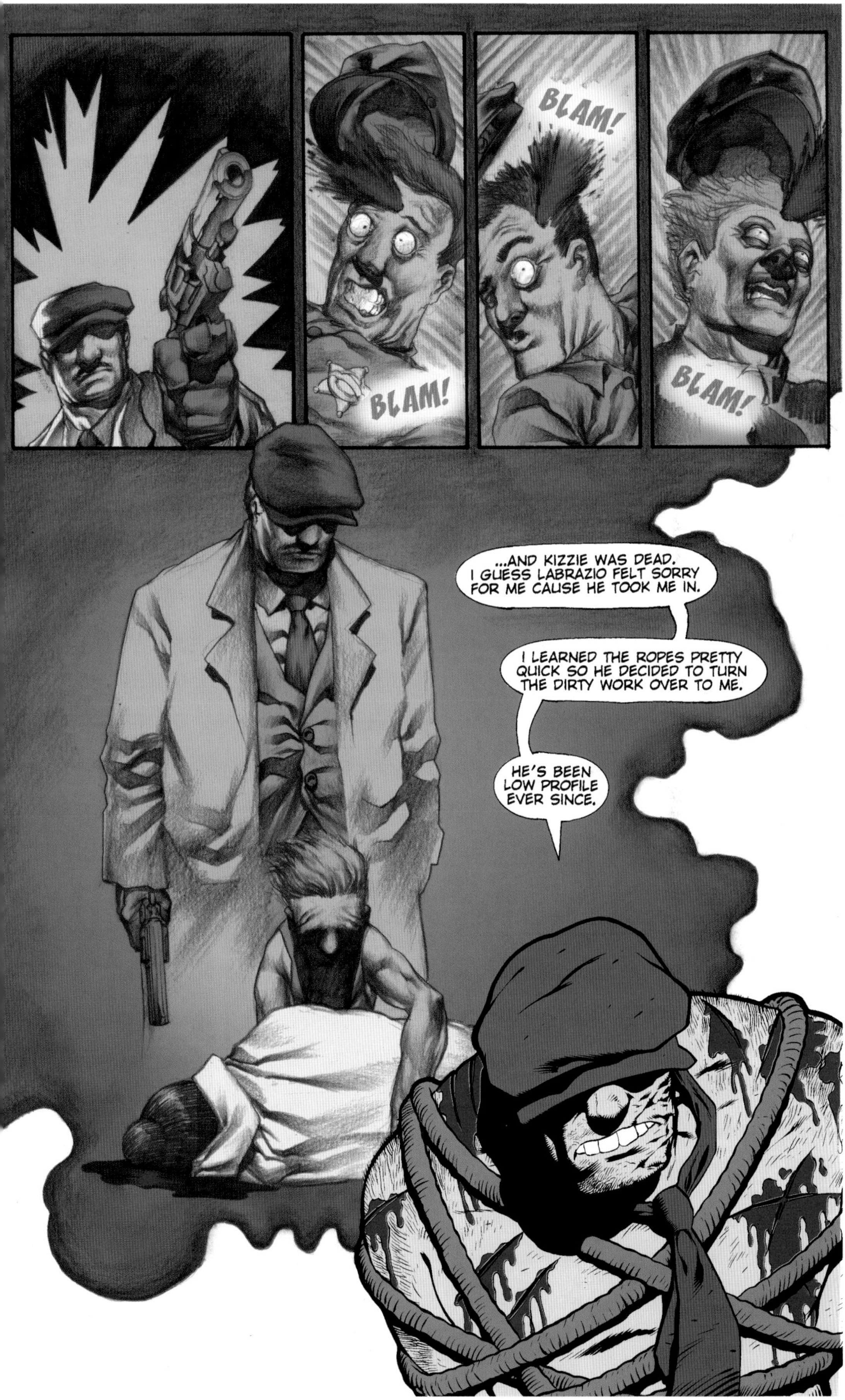
BLAM!
BLAM!
BLAM!
...AND KIZZIE WAS DEAD. I GUESS LABRAZIO FELT SORRY FOR ME CAUSE HE TOOK ME IN.
I LEARNED THE ROPES PRETTY QUICK SO HE DECIDED TO TURN THE DIRTY WORK OVER TO ME.
HE'S BEEN LOW PROFILE EVER SINCE.

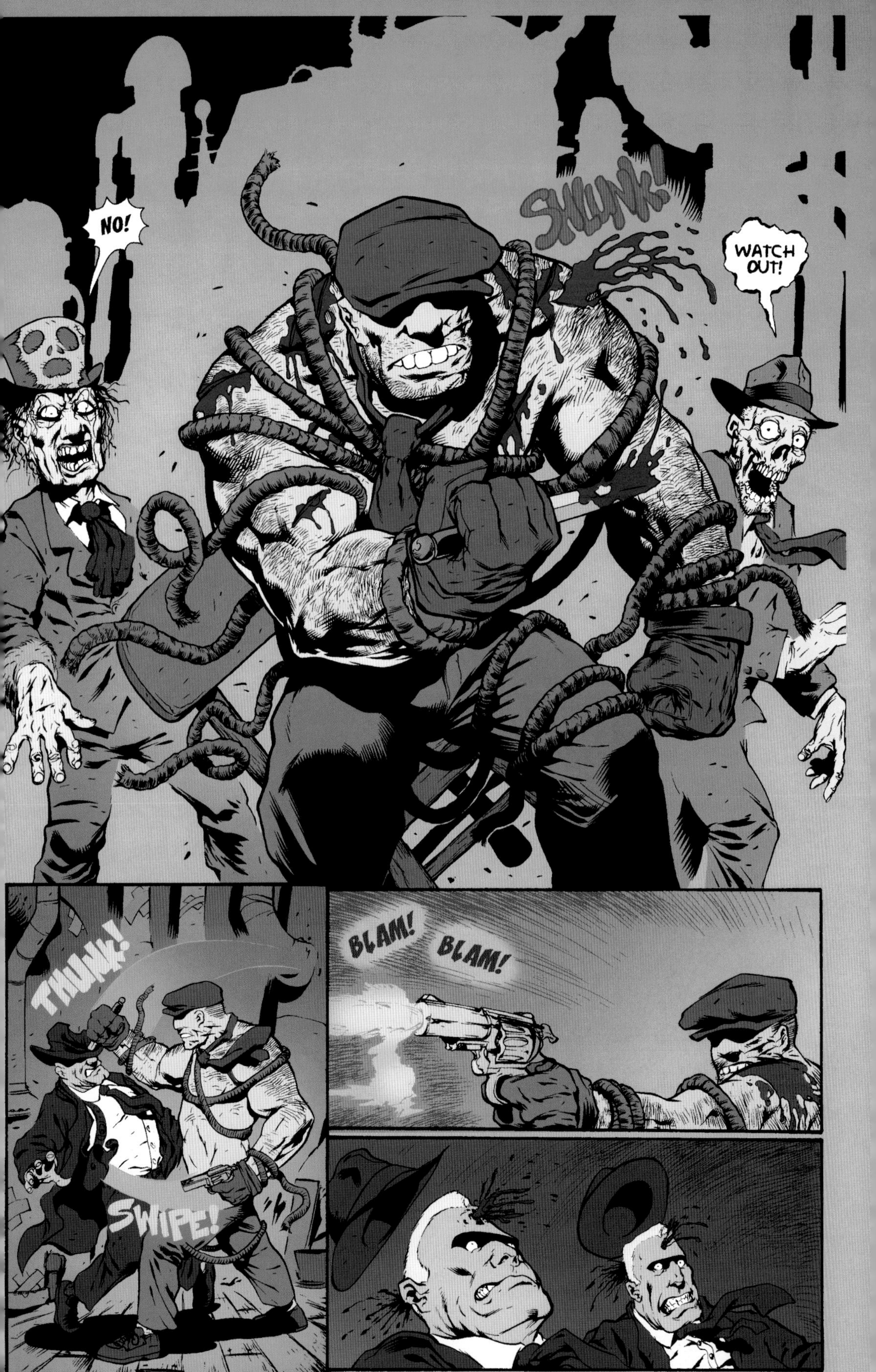
NO!
SHLUNK!
WATCH OUT!
THUNK!
SWIPE!
BLAM!
BLAM!

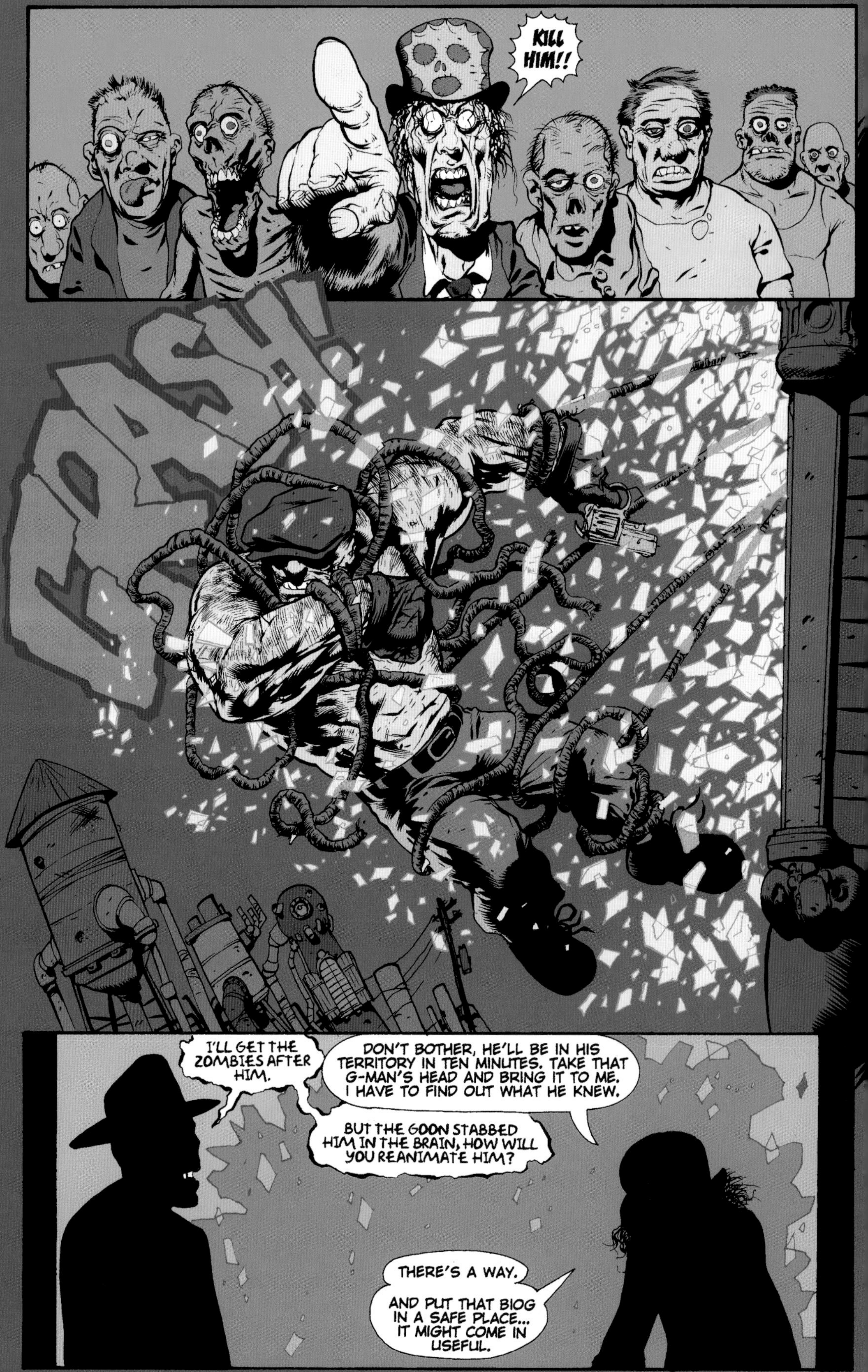
KILL HIM!!
I'LL GET THE ZOMBIES AFTER HIM.
DON'T BOTHER, HE'LL BE IN HIS TERRITORY IN TEN MINUTES. TAKE THAT G-MAN'S HEAD AND BRING IT TO ME. I HAVE TO FIND OUT WHAT HE KNEW.
BUT THE GOON STABBED HIM IN THE BRAIN, HOW WILL YOU REANIMATE HIM?
THERE'S A WAY.
AND PUT THAT BIOG IN A SAFE PLACE... IT MIGHT COME IN USEFUL.

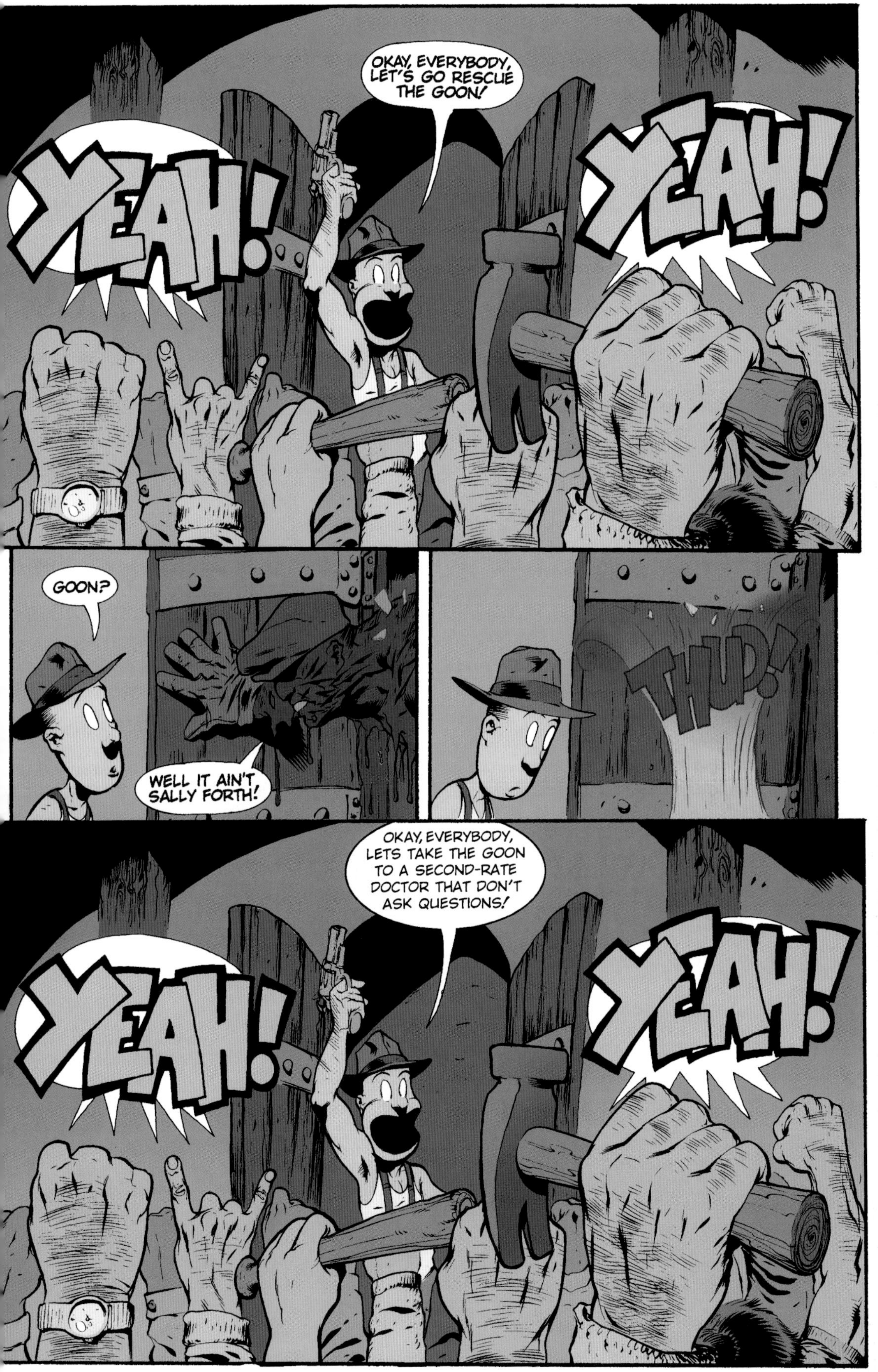
OKAY, EVERYBODY, LET'S GO RESCUE THE GOON!
YEAH!
YEAH!
GOON?
WELL IT AIN'T SALLY FORTH!
THUD!
OKAY, EVERYBODY, LETS TAKE THE GOON TO A SECOND-RATE DOCTOR THAT DON'T ASK QUESTIONS!
YEAH!
YEAH!

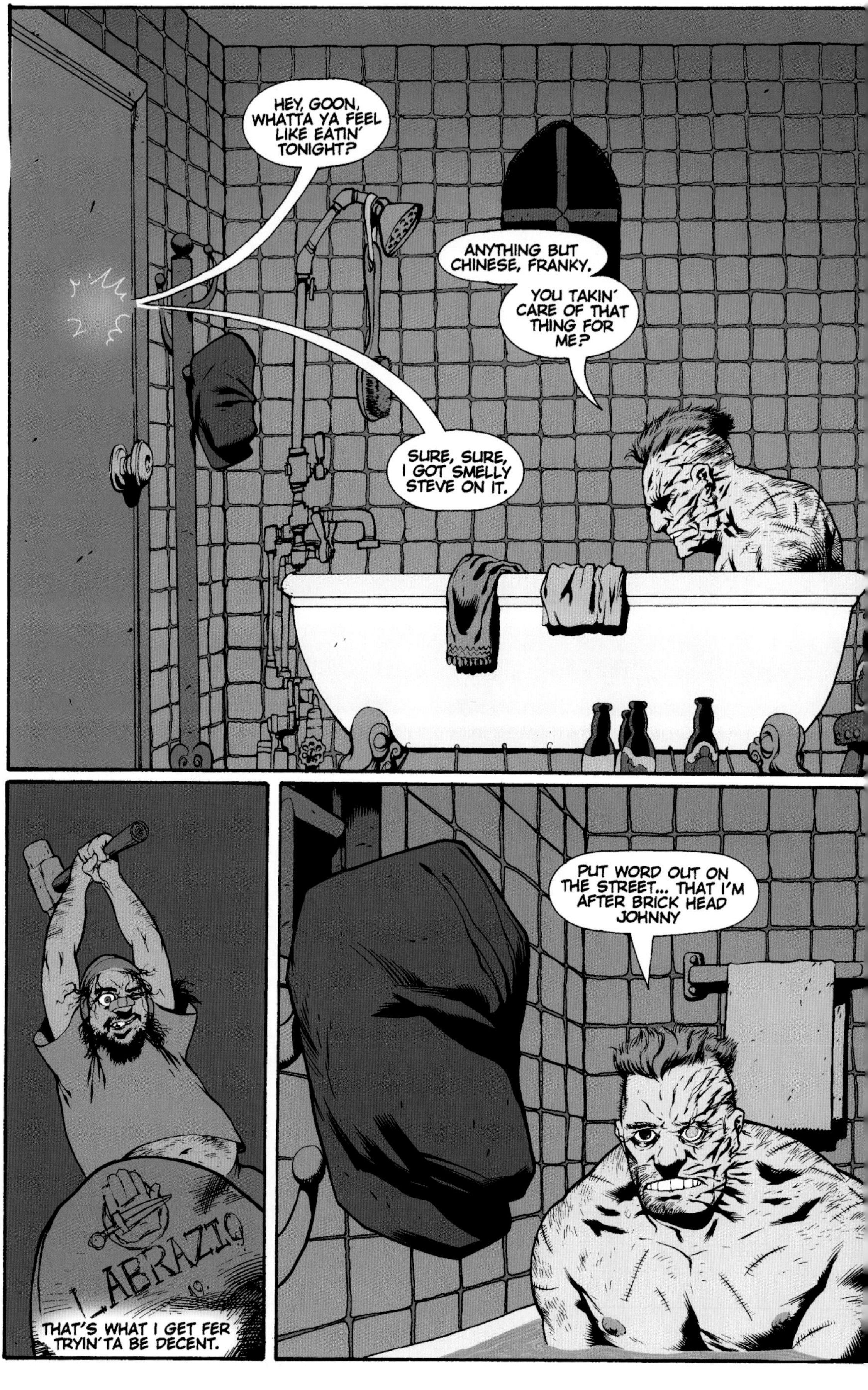
HEY, GOON, WHATTA YA FEEL LIKE EATIN' TONIGHT?
ANYTHING BUT CHINESE, FRANKY.
YOU TAKIN' CARE OF THAT THING FOR ME?
SURE, SURE, I GOT SMELLY STEVE ON IT.
ABRAZIO
THAT'S WHAT I GET FER TRYIN'TA BE DECENT.
PUT WORD OUT ON THE STREET... THAT I'M AFTER BRICK HEAD JOHNNY

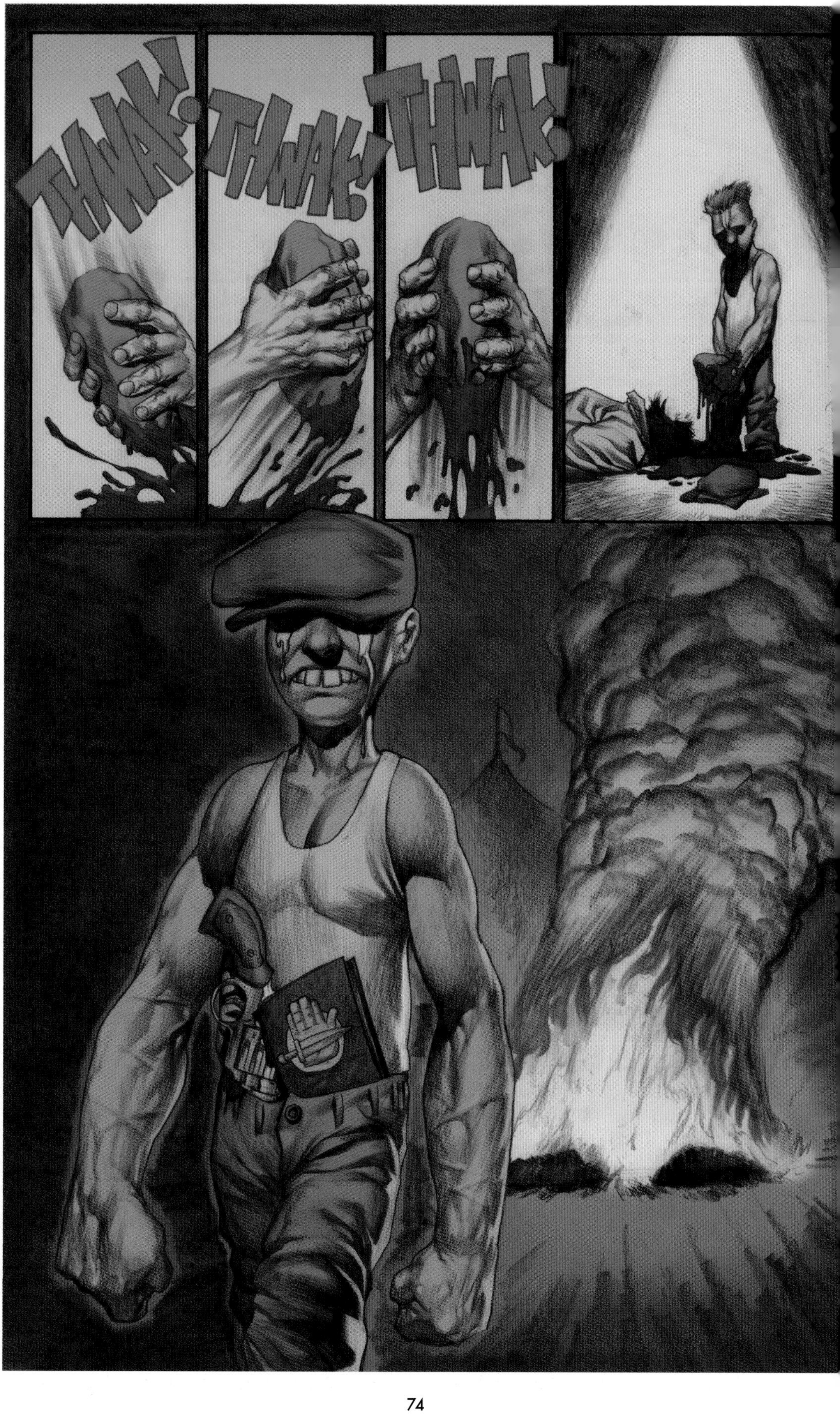
THWAK!
THWAK!
THWAK!

# THE GOON

## STRIPS

*Originally presented on thegoon.com*

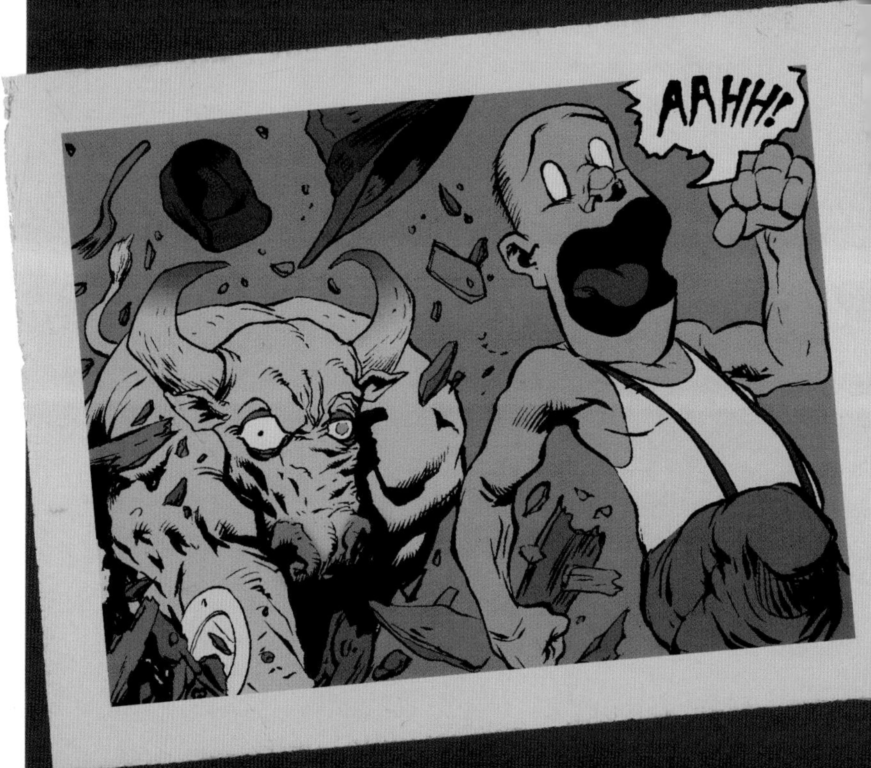
AAHH!

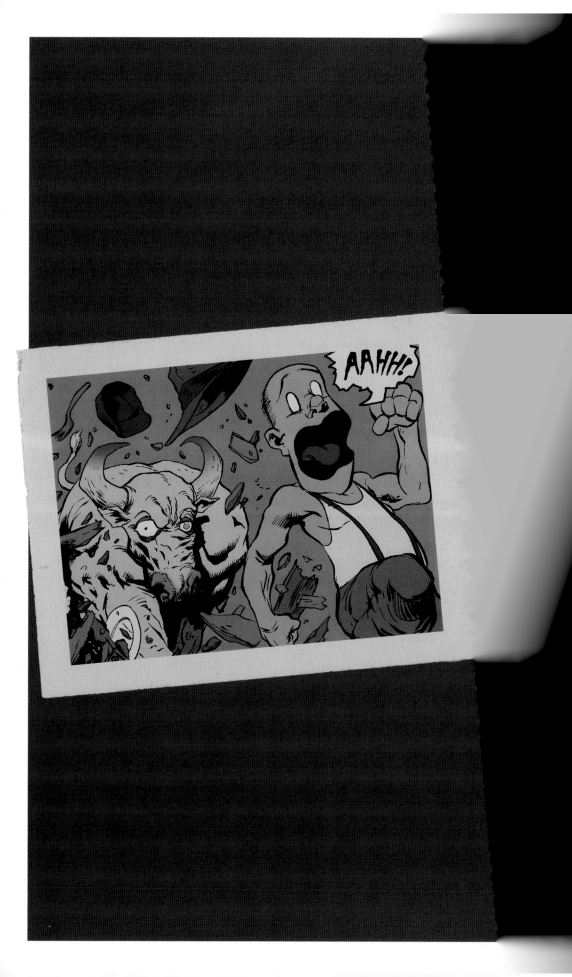

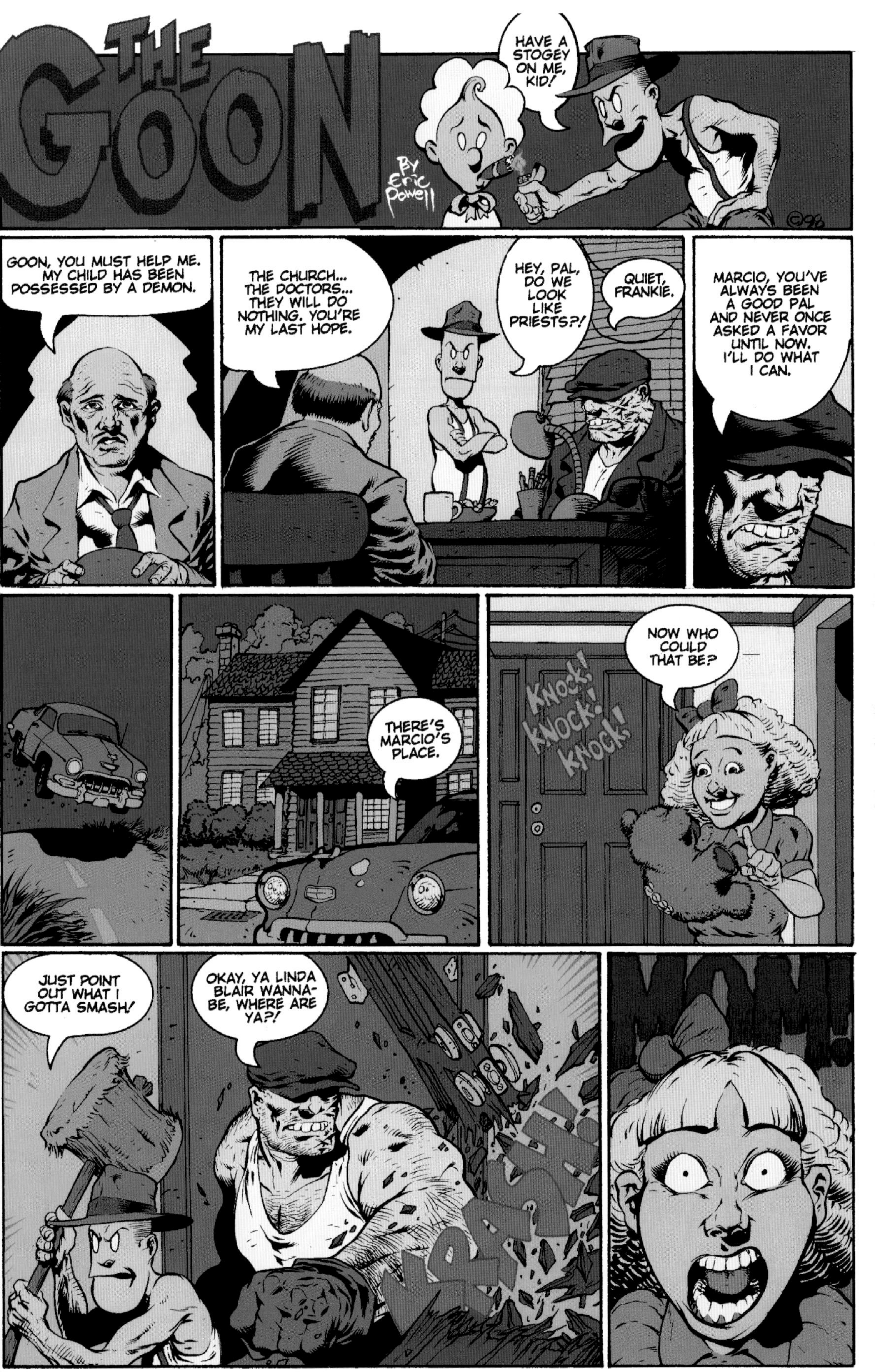
THE GOON
By Eric Powell
HAVE A STOGEY ON ME, KID!
©98
GOON, YOU MUST HELP ME. MY CHILD HAS BEEN POSSESSED BY A DEMON.
THE CHURCH... THE DOCTORS... THEY WILL DO NOTHING. YOU'RE MY LAST HOPE.
HEY, PAL, DO WE LOOK LIKE PRIESTS?!
QUIET, FRANKIE.
MARCIO, YOU'VE ALWAYS BEEN A GOOD PAL AND NEVER ONCE ASKED A FAVOR UNTIL NOW. I'LL DO WHAT I CAN.
THERE'S MARCIO'S PLACE.
KNOCK! KNOCK! KNOCK!
NOW WHO COULD THAT BE?
JUST POINT OUT WHAT I GOTTA SMASH!
OKAY, YA LINDA BLAIR WANNA-BE, WHERE ARE YA?!
KRASH!
MOM!

# THE GOON™

## SKETCHBOOK

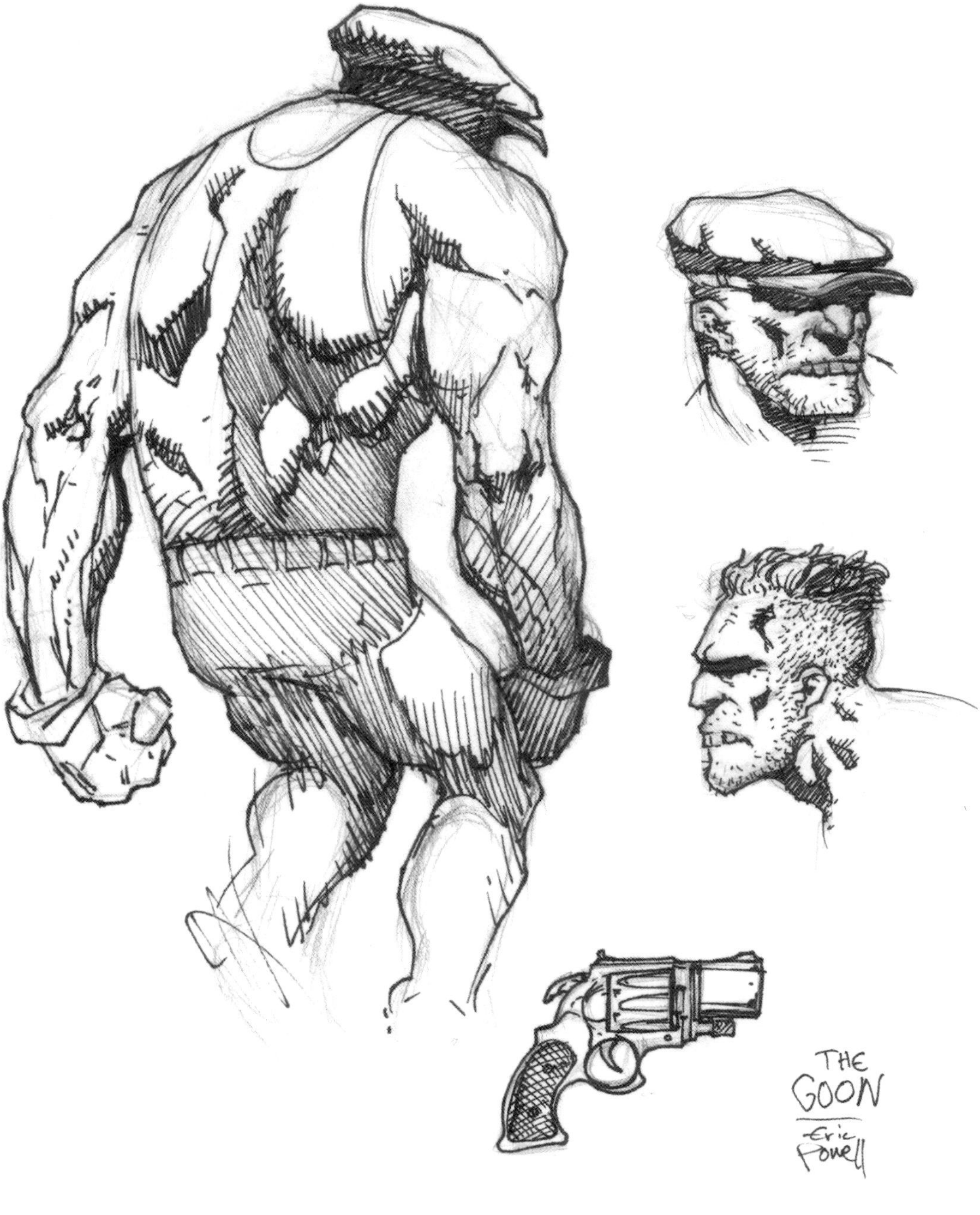
THE GOON
Eric Powell

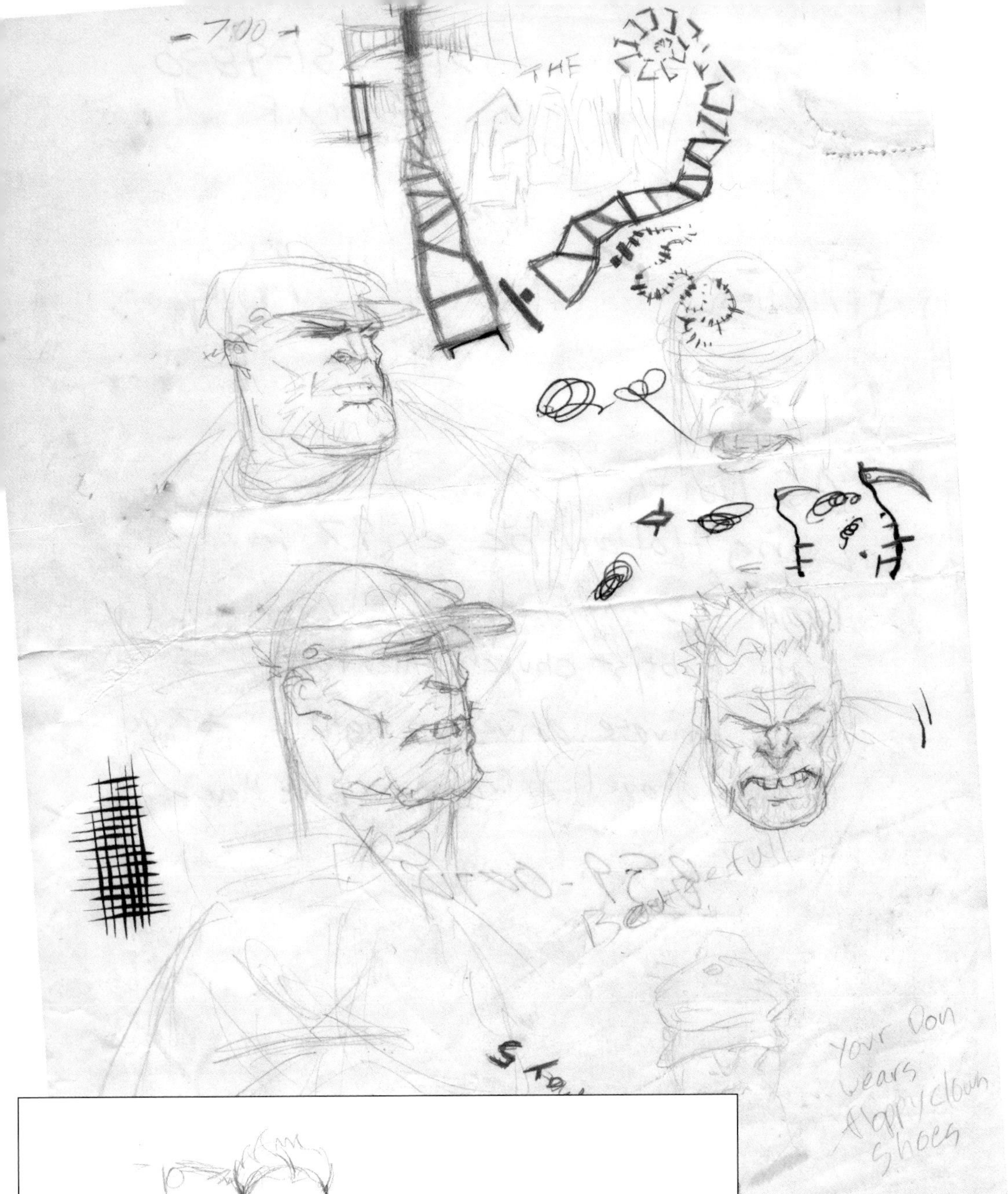
THE
Your Don
wears
floppyclown
Shoes

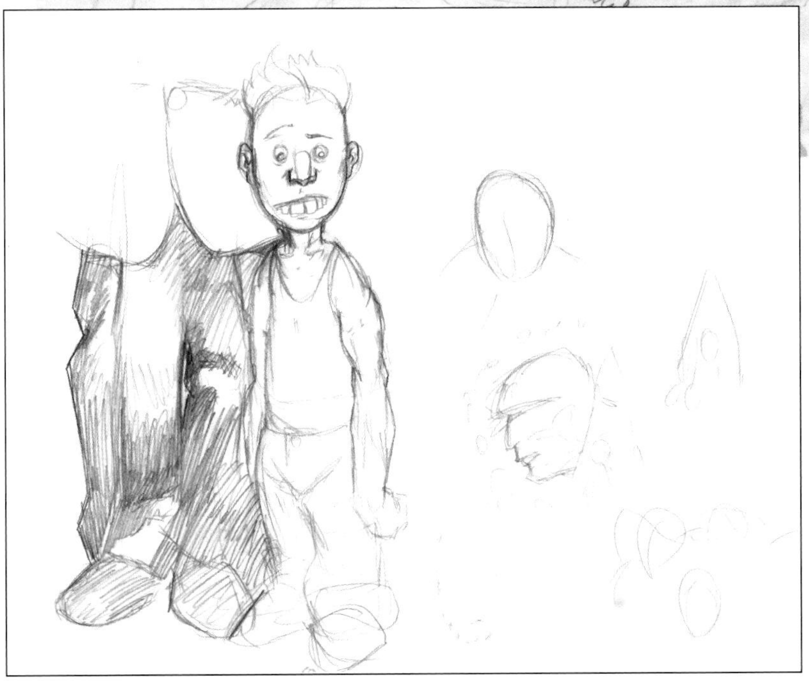

Above: the first Goon drawing.
Left: early Goon scribbles.

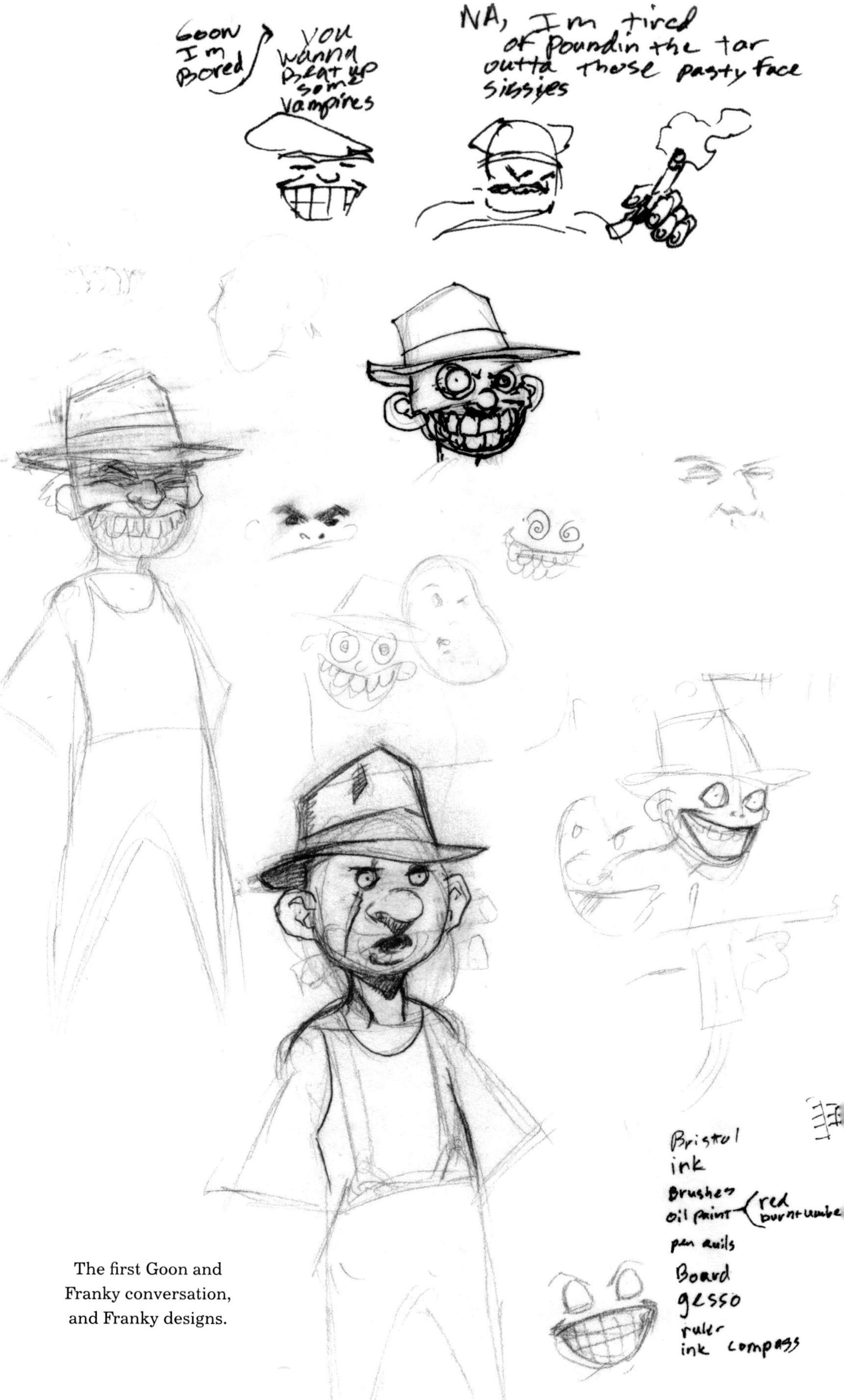
Goon I'm Bored
you wanna beat up some vampires
NA, I'm tired of poundin the tar outta these pasty face sissies
Bristol
ink
Brushes
oil paint
red
burnt umbe
pen nails
Board
gesso
ruler
ink compass

The first Goon and Franky conversation, and Franky designs.

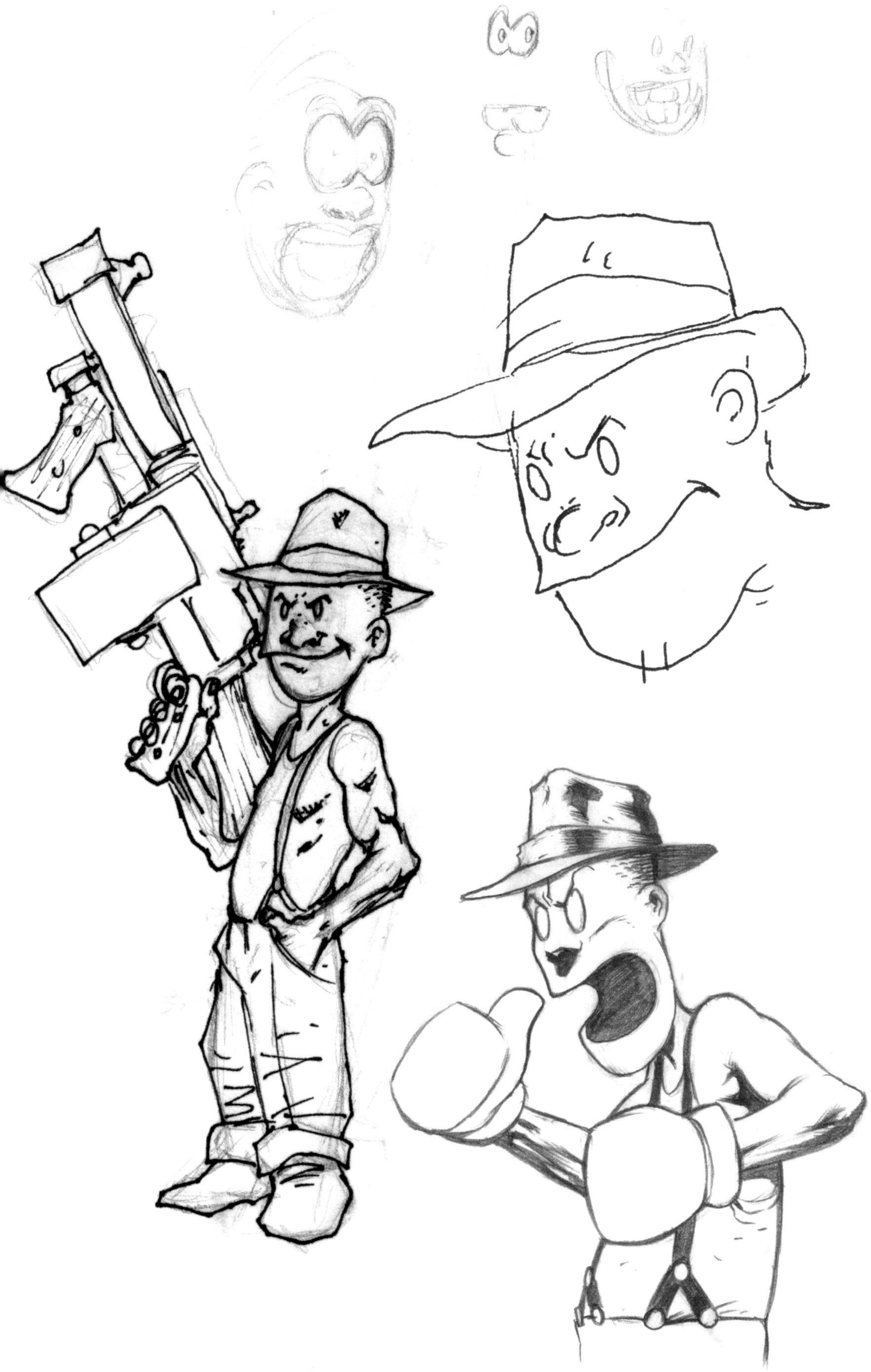

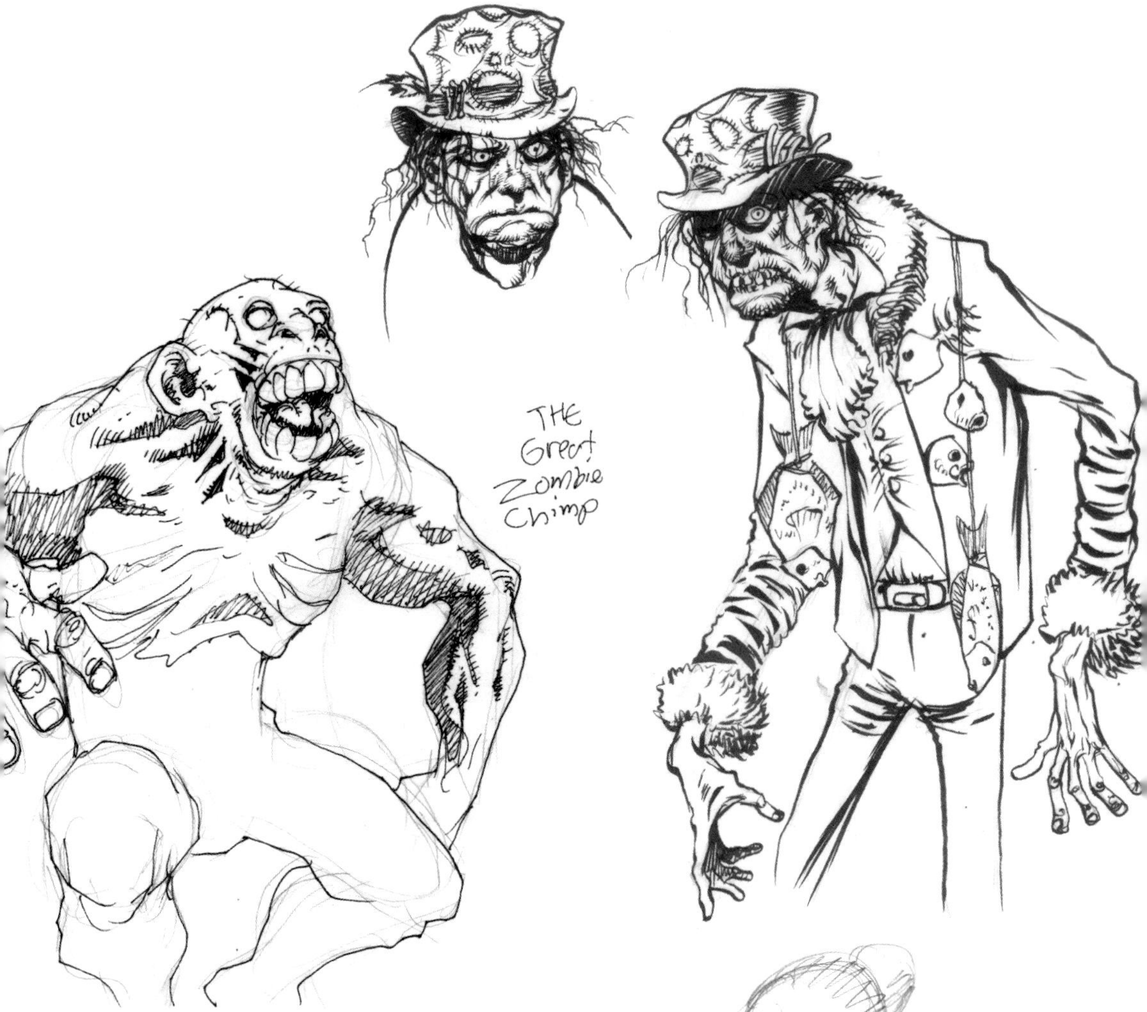
THE Great Zombie Chimp

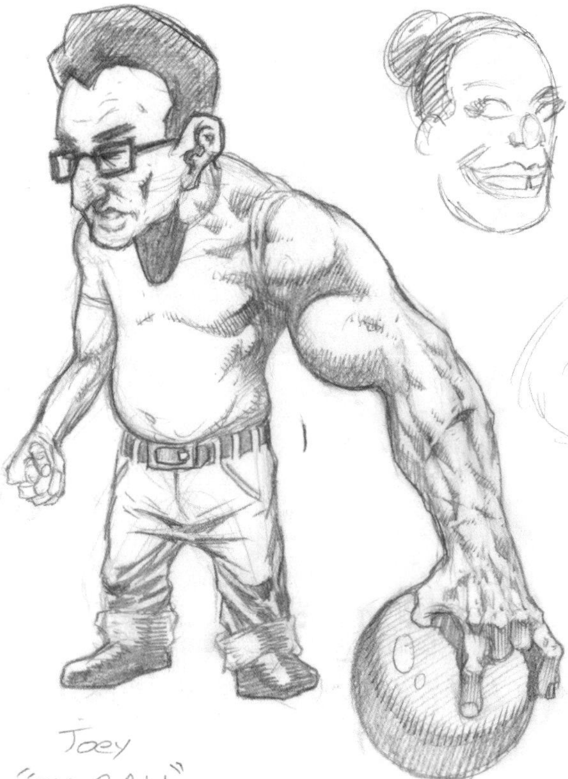
Joey
"THE BALL"

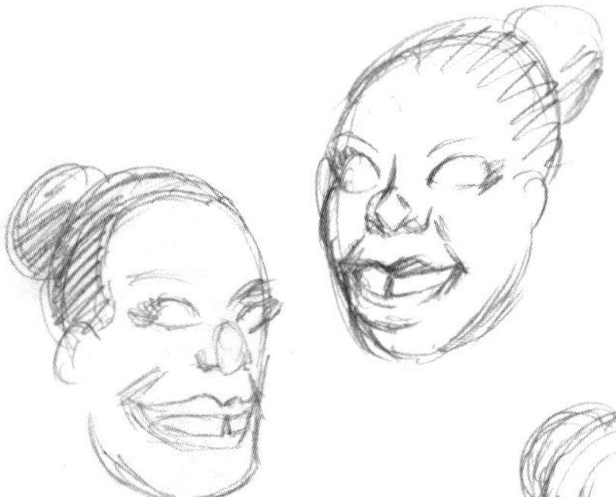

Aunt Kizzie sketch.

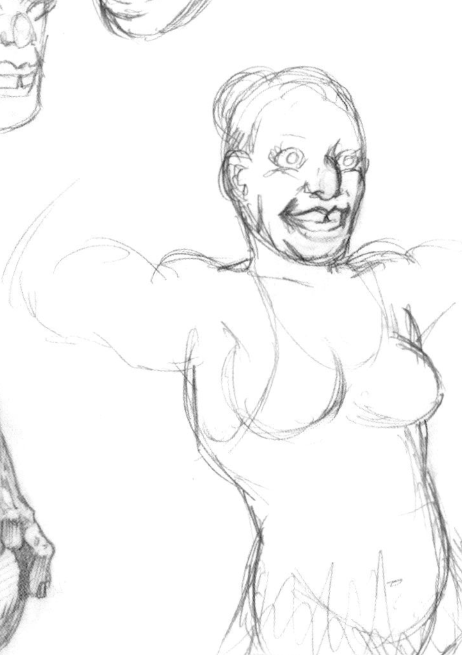

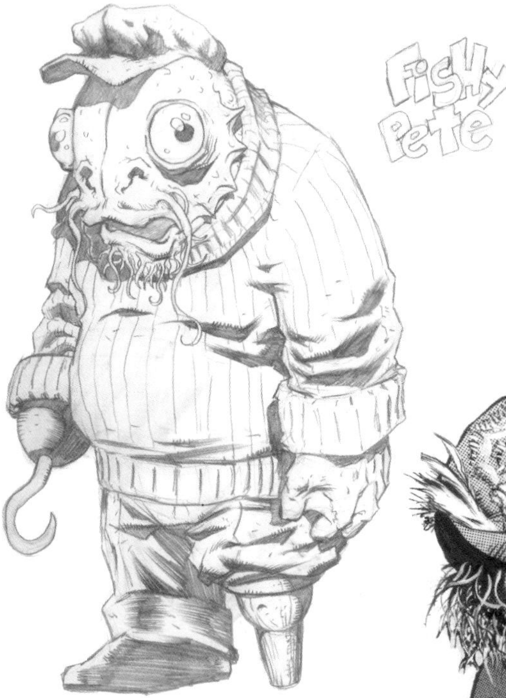
Fishy Pete

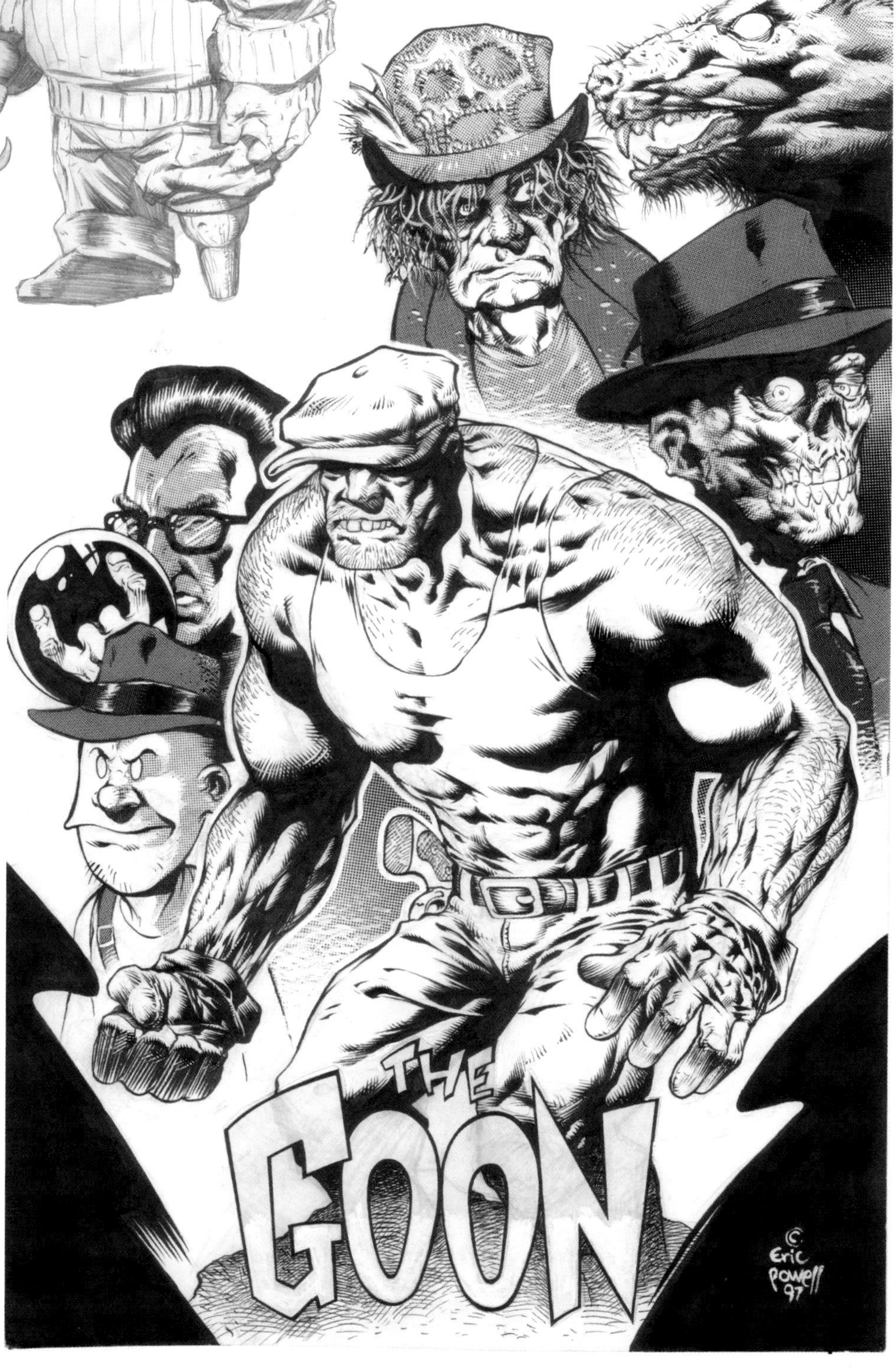
THE GOON
© Eric Powell 97

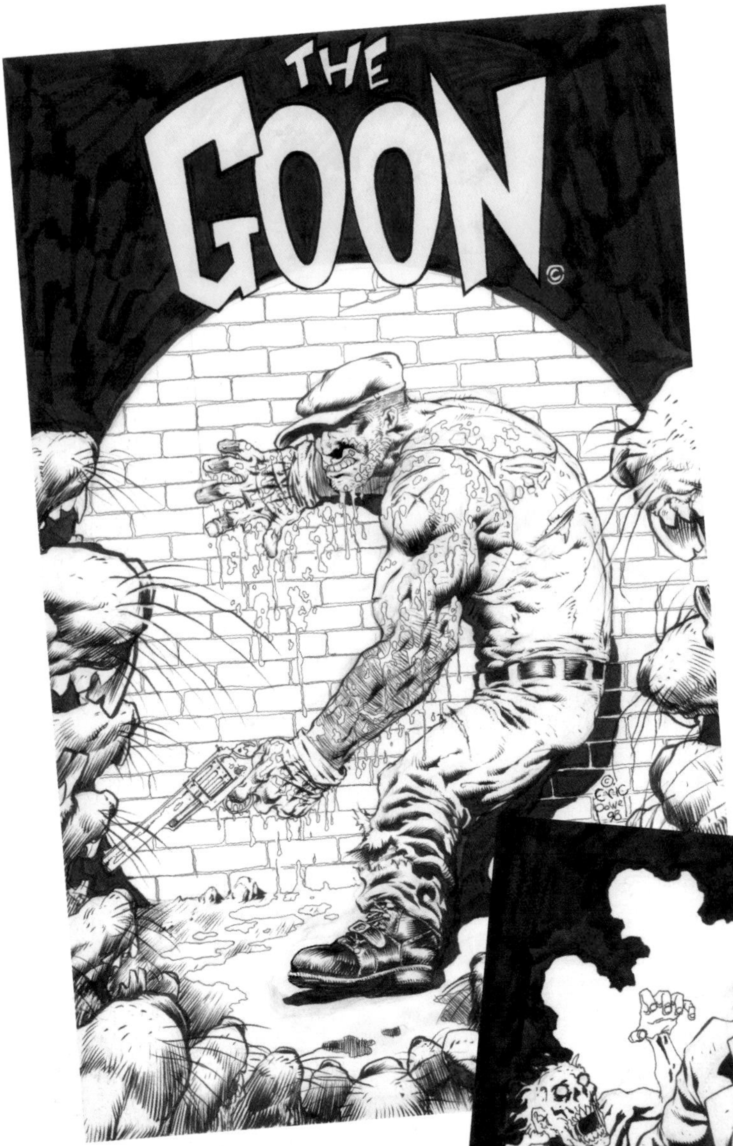
THE
GOON ©
Eric Powell 98

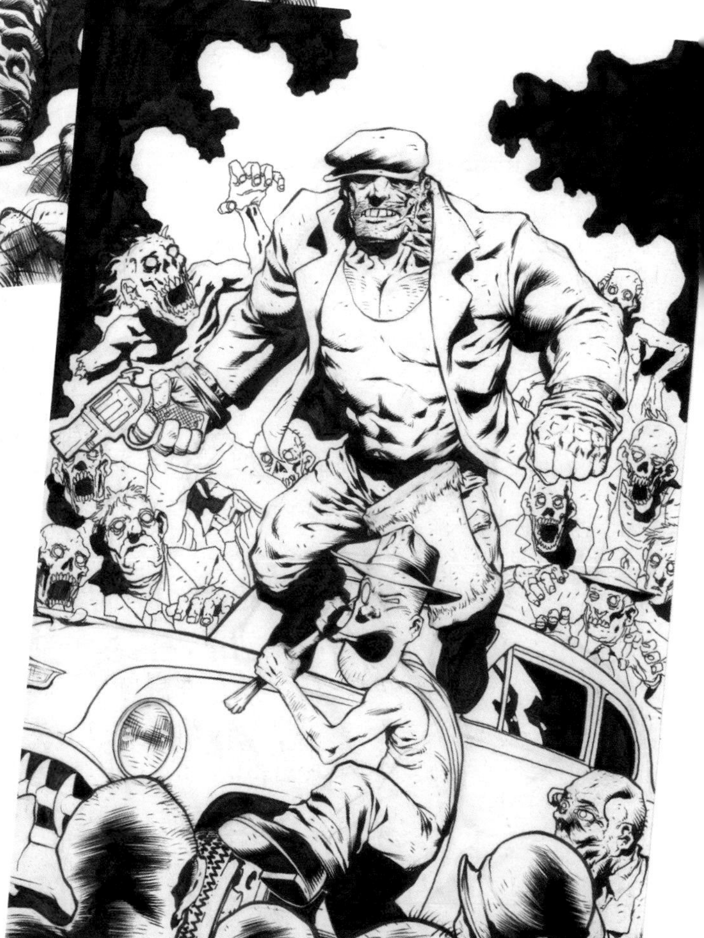
Eric Powell 98

The following two pages are the beginning of the first *Goon* story (unfinished).

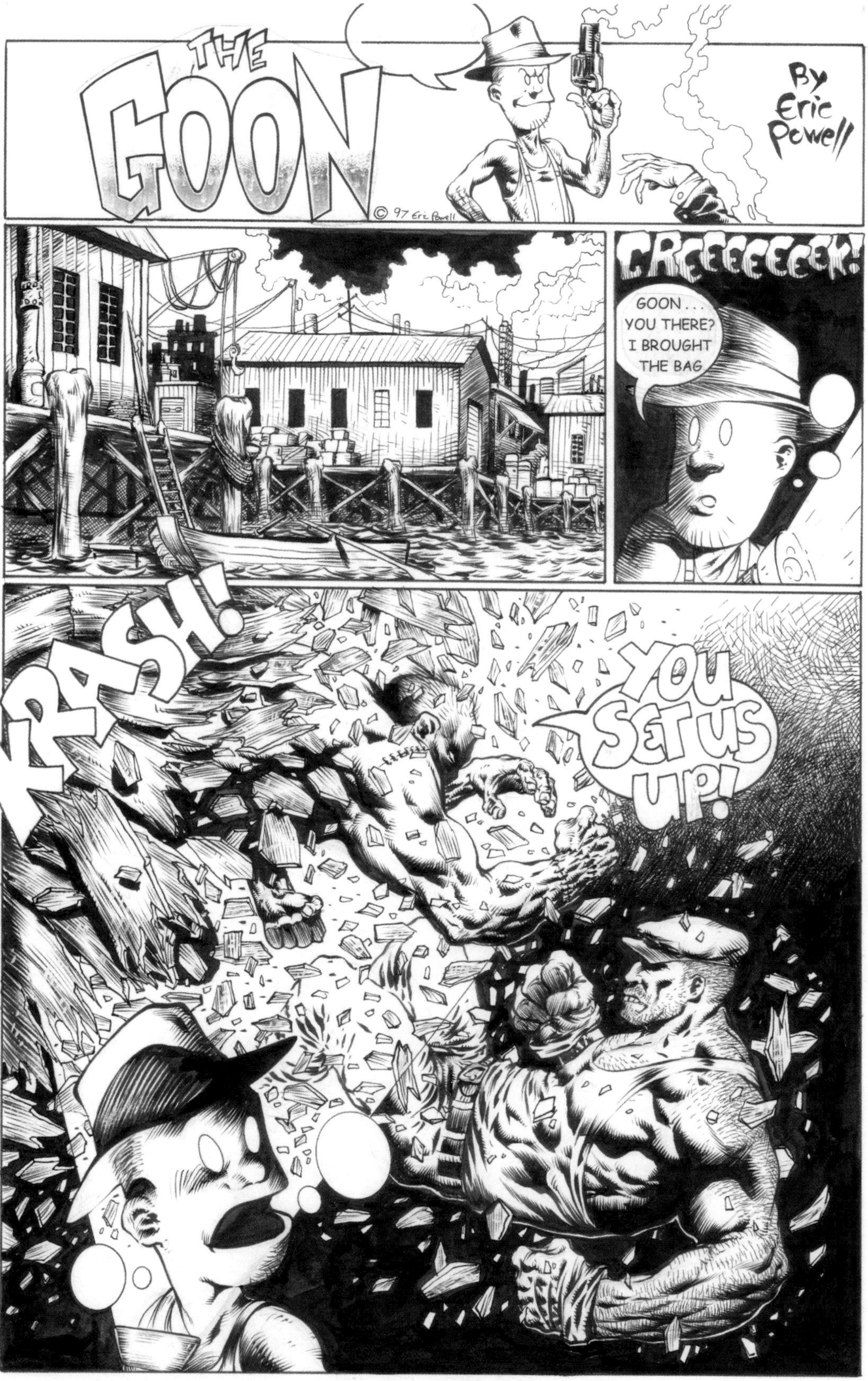
THE GOON
By Eric Powell
© 97 Eric Powell
CREEEEEEEK!
GOON... YOU THERE? I BROUGHT THE BAG
KRASH!
YOU SET US UP!

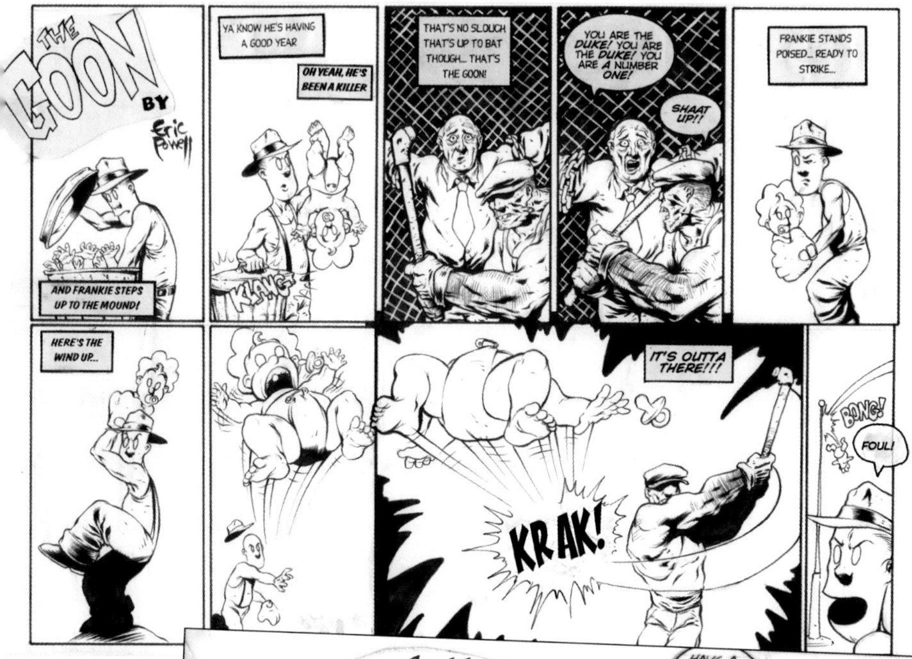
THE GOON
BY Eric Powell
AND FRANKIE STEPS UP TO THE MOUND!
YA KNOW HE'S HAVING A GOOD YEAR
OH YEAH, HE'S BEEN A KILLER
KLANG
THAT'S NO SLOUCH THAT'S UP TO BAT THOUGH... THAT'S THE GOON!
YOU ARE THE DUKE! YOU ARE THE DUKE! YOU ARE A NUMBER ONE!
SHAAT UP!!
FRANKIE STANDS POISED... READY TO STRIKE...
HERE'S THE WIND UP...
IT'S OUTTA THERE!!!
KRAK!
BONG!
FOUL!

Early unused strip. At the time I thought playing baseball with babies might have been too harsh.

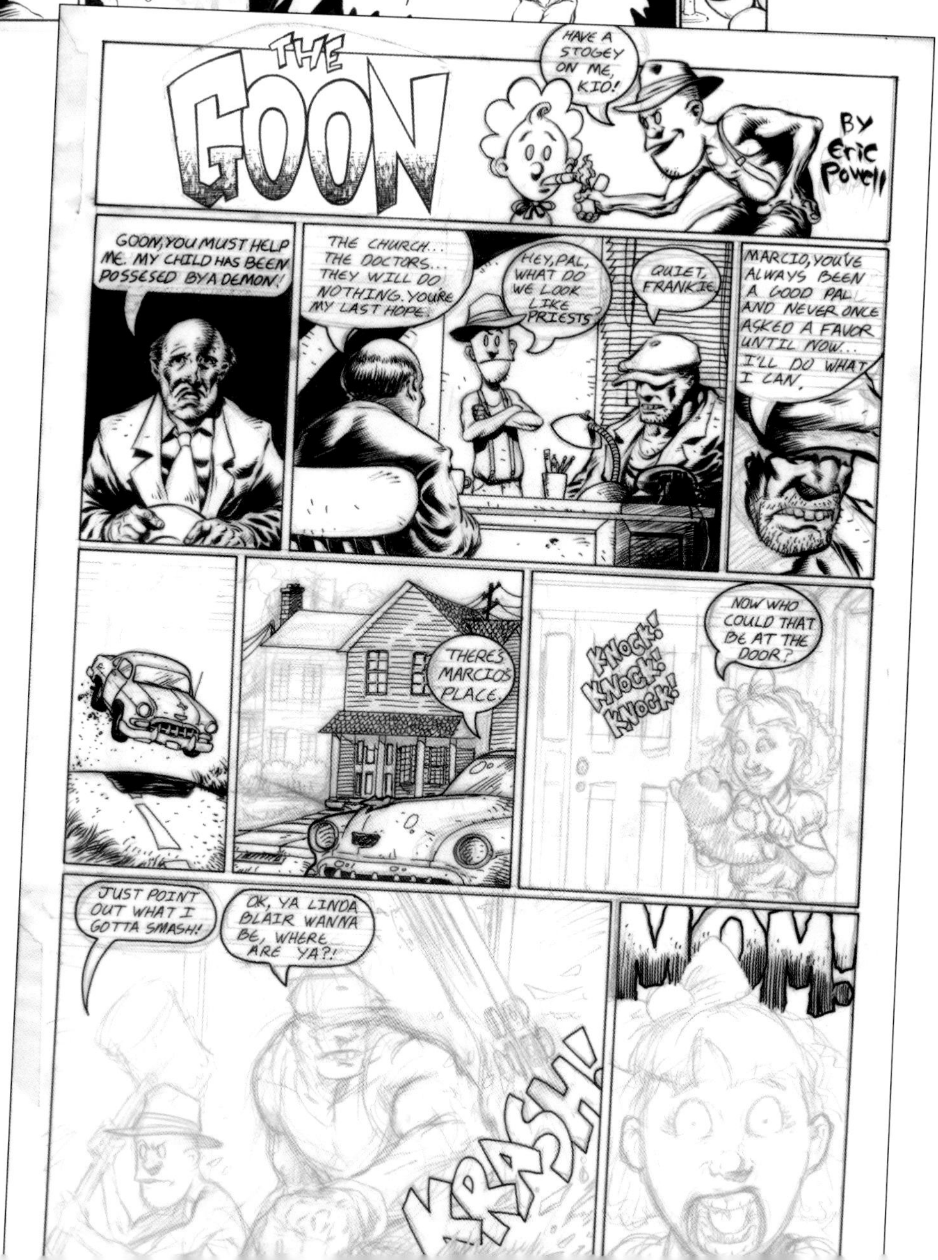
THE GOON
HAVE A STOGEY ON ME, KID!
By Eric Powell
GOON, YOU MUST HELP ME. MY CHILD HAS BEEN POSSESSED BY A DEMON!
THE CHURCH... THE DOCTORS... THEY WILL DO NOTHING. YOU'RE MY LAST HOPE.
HEY, PAL, WHAT DO WE LOOK LIKE PRIESTS?
QUIET, FRANKIE.
MARCIO, YOU'VE ALWAYS BEEN A GOOD PAL AND NEVER ONCE ASKED A FAVOR UNTIL NOW... I'LL DO WHAT I CAN.
THERE'S MARCIO'S PLACE.
KNOCK! KNOCK! KNOCK!
NOW WHO COULD THAT BE AT THE DOOR?
JUST POINT OUT WHAT I GOTTA SMASH!
OK, YA LINDA BLAIR WANNA BE, WHERE ARE YA?!
KRASH!
MOM!

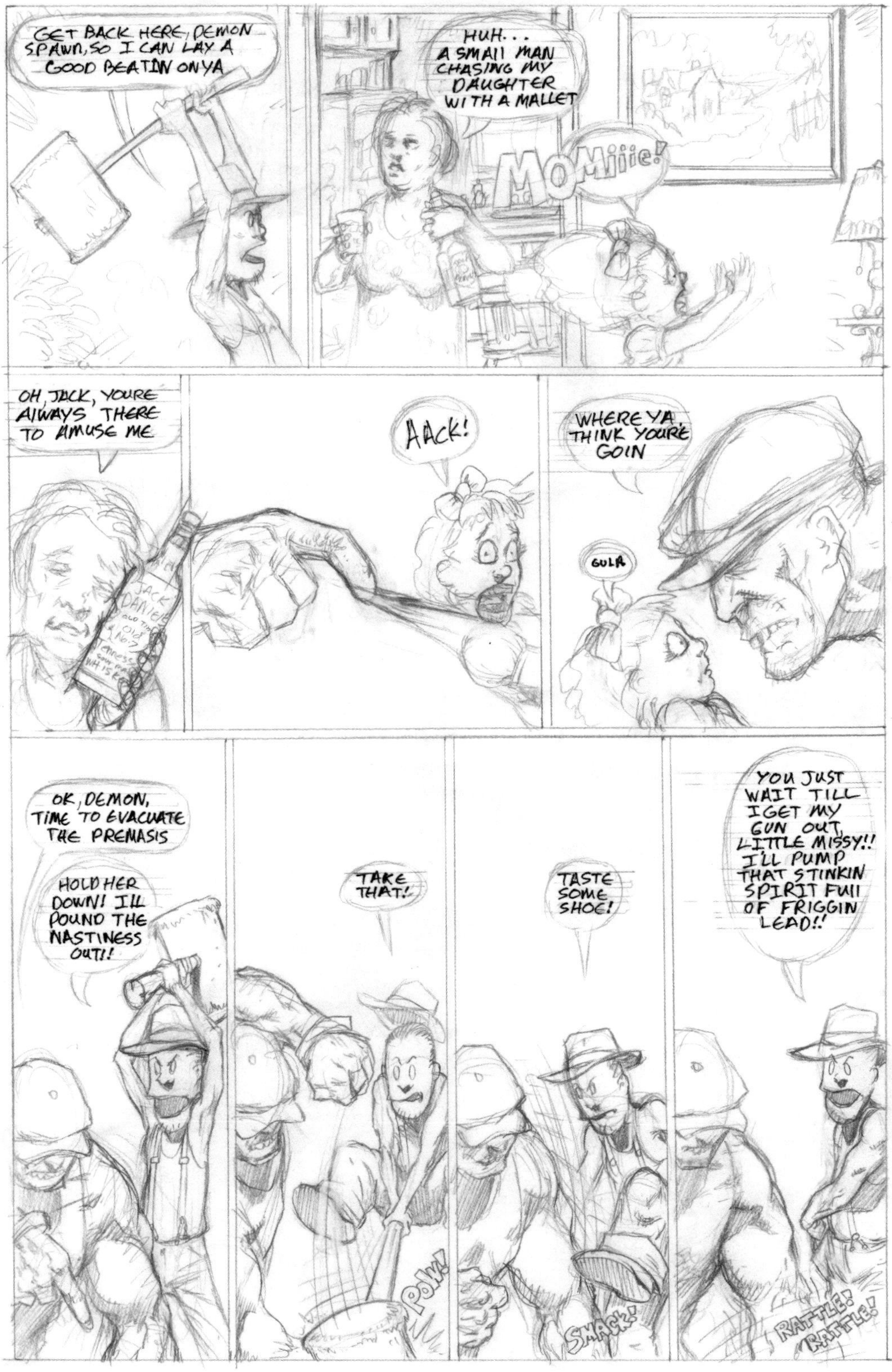
GET BACK HERE, DEMON SPAWN, SO I CAN LAY A GOOD BEATIN ONYA
HUH... A SMAll MAN CHASING MY DAUGHTER WITH A MALLET
MOMiiie!
OH, JACK, YOURE ALWAYS THERE TO AMUSE ME
JACK DANIEL'S
AACK!
WHERE YA THINK YOURE GOIN
GULP
OK, DEMON, TIME TO EVACUATE THE PREMASIS
HOLD HER DOWN! I'LL POUND THE NASTINESS OUT!!
TAKE THAT!
POW!
TASTE SOME SHOE!
SMACK!
YOU JUST WAIT TILL I GET MY GUN OUT, LITTLE MISSY!! I'LL PUMP THAT STINKIN SPIRIT FUll OF FRIGGIN LEAD!!
RATTLE! RATTLE!

2

GOON BACKUP #2 page 2

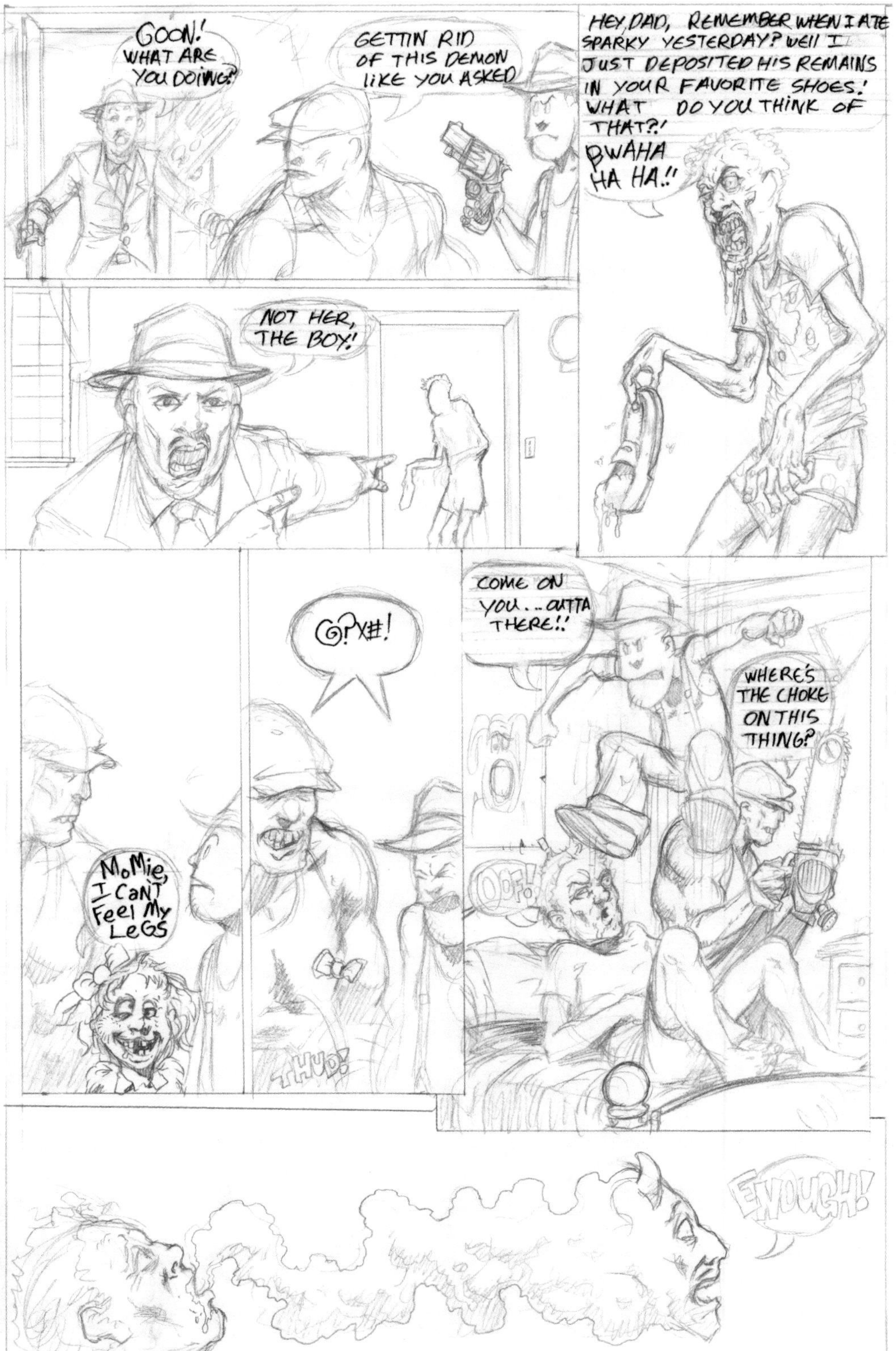
GOON! WHAT ARE YOU DOING?
GETTIN RID OF THIS DEMON LIKE YOU ASKED
HEY, DAD, REMEMBER WHEN I ATE SPARKY YESTERDAY? WELL I JUST DEPOSITED HIS REMAINS IN YOUR FAVORITE SHOES! WHAT DO YOU THINK OF THAT?!
BWAHA HA HA!!
NOT HER, THE BOY!
MoMie, I CaN'T Feel My LeGS
@?x#!
THUD!
COME ON YOU... OUTTA THERE!!
WHERE'S THE CHOKE ON THIS THING?
OOF!
ENOUGH!

5

GOON BACK UP #2 PAGE 3

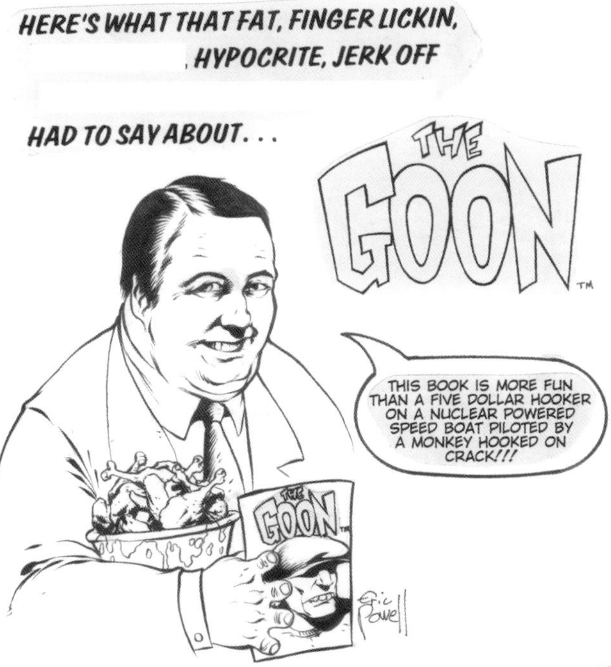
HERE'S WHAT THAT FAT, FINGER LICKIN,
, HYPOCRITE, JERK OFF
HAD TO SAY ABOUT . . .
THE GOON™
THIS BOOK IS MORE FUN THAN A FIVE DOLLAR HOOKER ON A NUCLEAR POWERED SPEED BOAT PILOTED BY A MONKEY HOOKED ON CRACK!!!
THE GOON™
Eric Powell

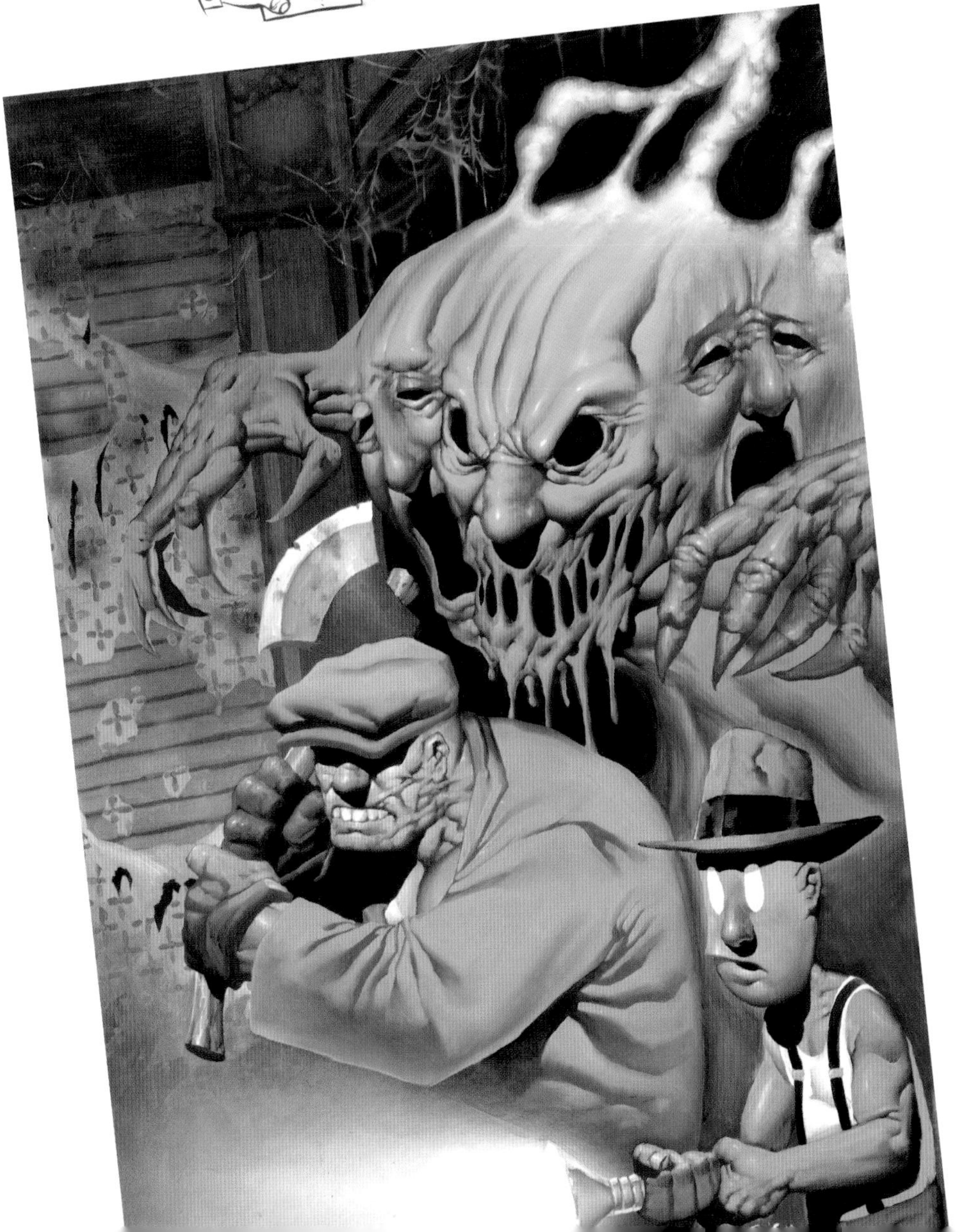

Left: unused ad.
Below: unused cover art.

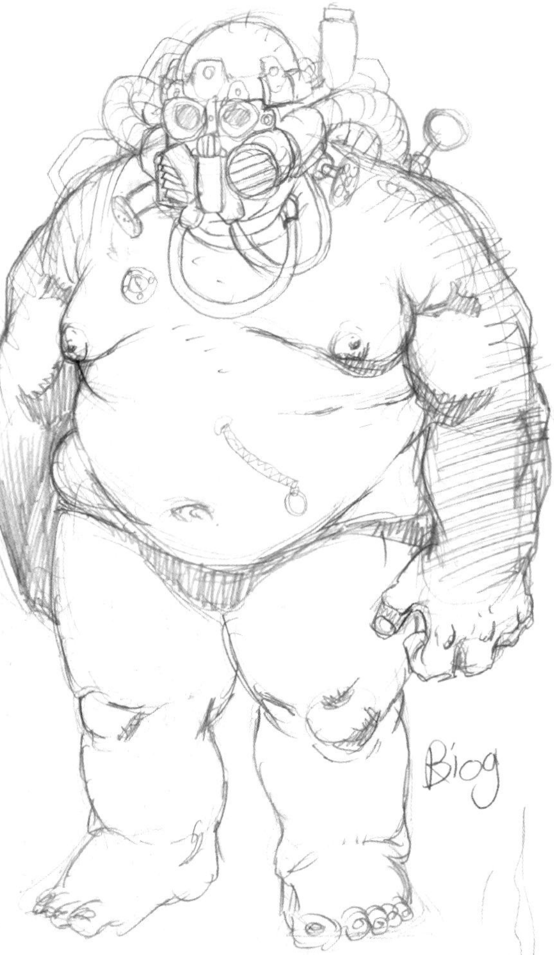
Blog

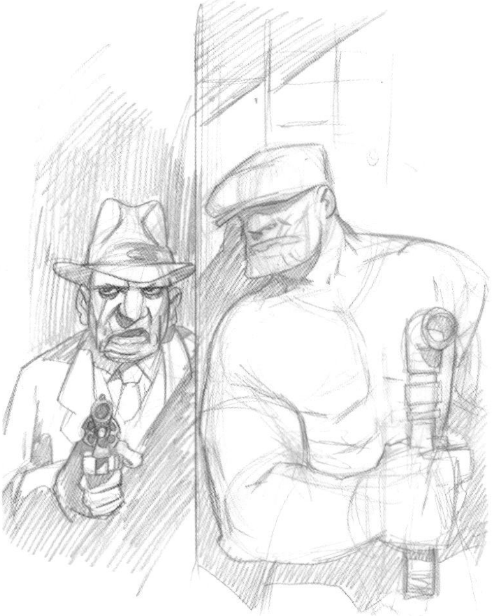

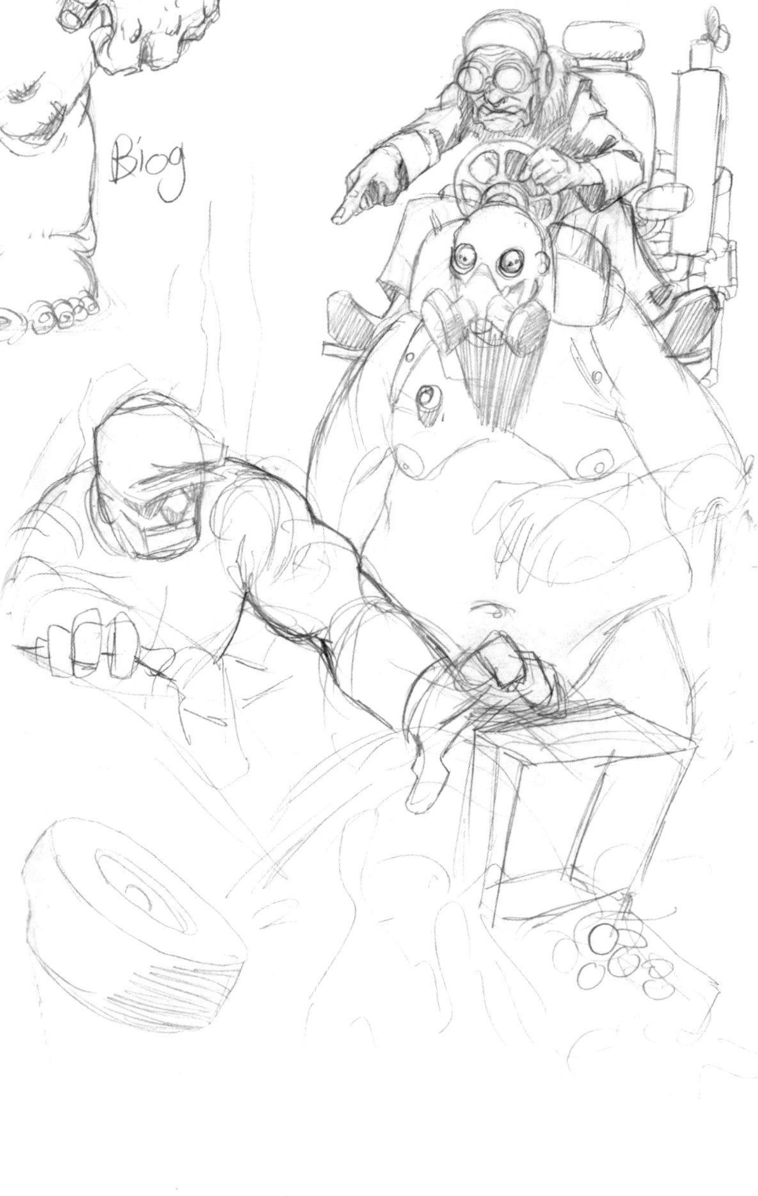

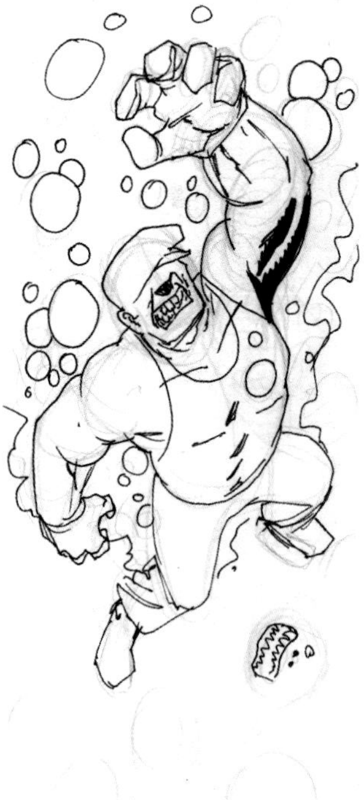

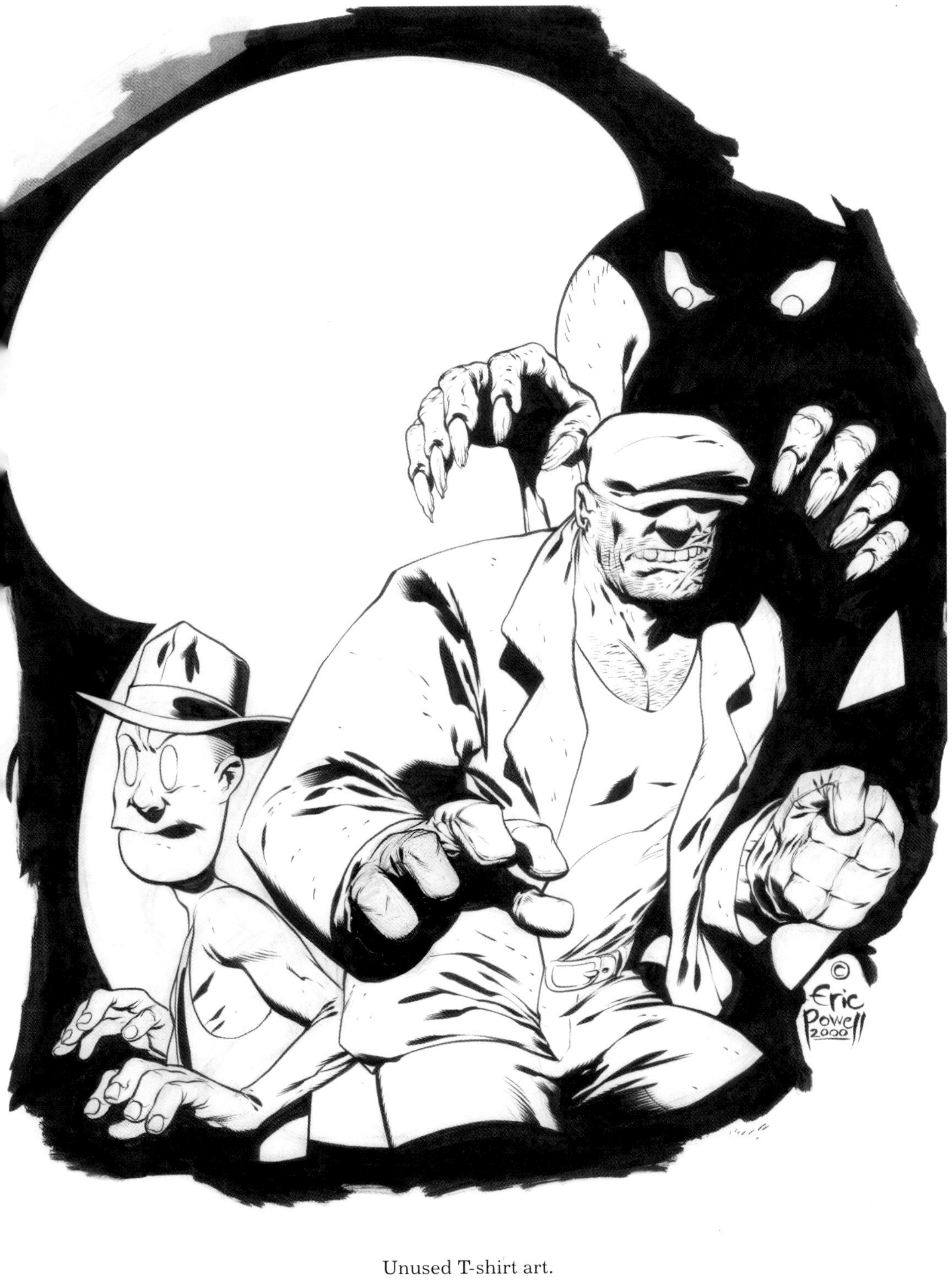
©
Eric
Powell
2000

Unused T-shirt art.

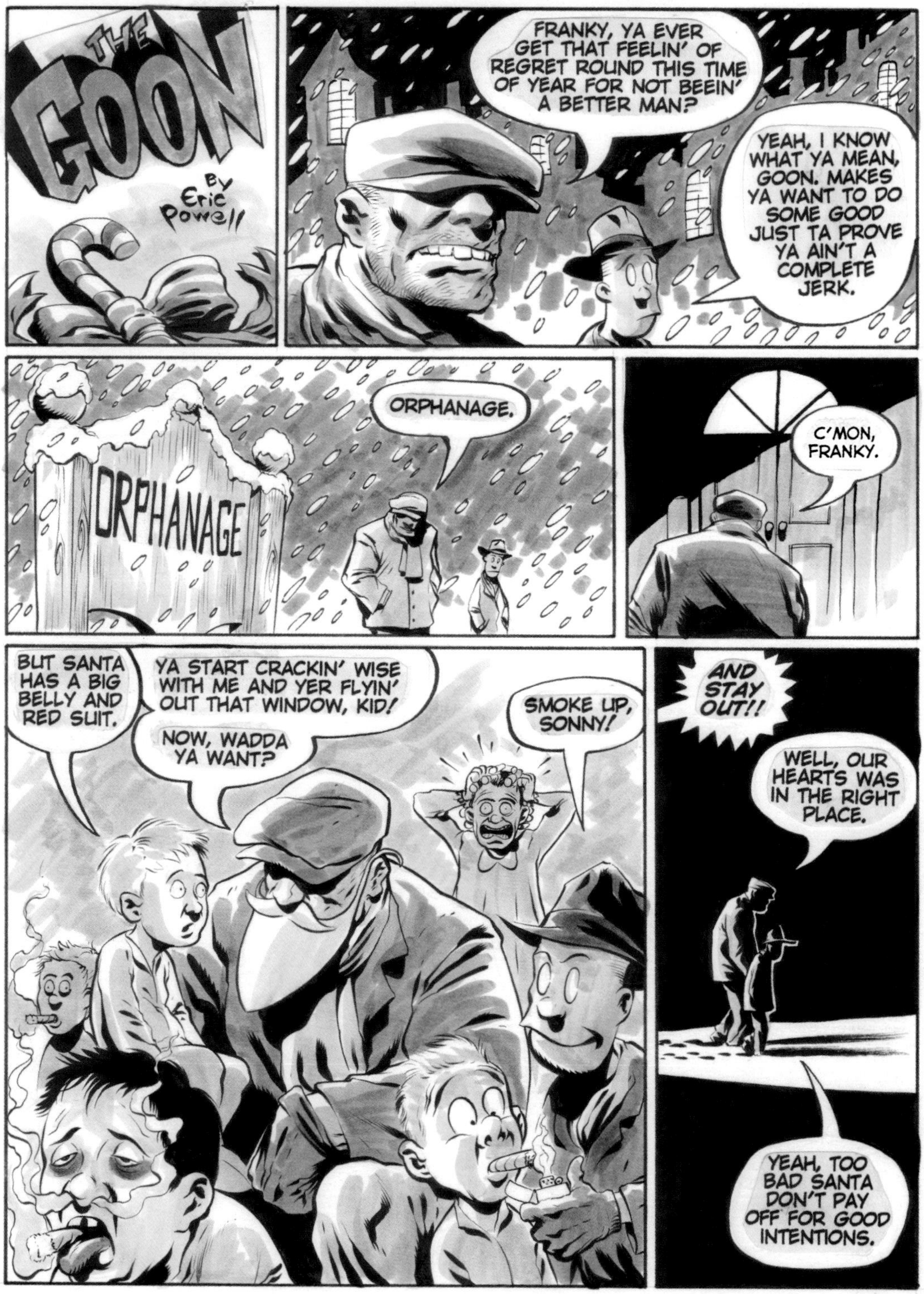
THE GOON
By Eric Powell
FRANKY, YA EVER GET THAT FEELIN' OF REGRET ROUND THIS TIME OF YEAR FOR NOT BEEIN' A BETTER MAN?
YEAH, I KNOW WHAT YA MEAN, GOON. MAKES YA WANT TO DO SOME GOOD JUST TA PROVE YA AIN'T A COMPLETE JERK.
ORPHANAGE
ORPHANAGE.
C'MON, FRANKY.
BUT SANTA HAS A BIG BELLY AND RED SUIT.
YA START CRACKIN' WISE WITH ME AND YER FLYIN' OUT THAT WINDOW, KID!
NOW, WADDA YA WANT?
SMOKE UP, SONNY!
AND STAY OUT!!
WELL, OUR HEARTS WAS IN THE RIGHT PLACE.
YEAH, TOO BAD SANTA DON'T PAY OFF FOR GOOD INTENTIONS.

Unused Christmas strip.

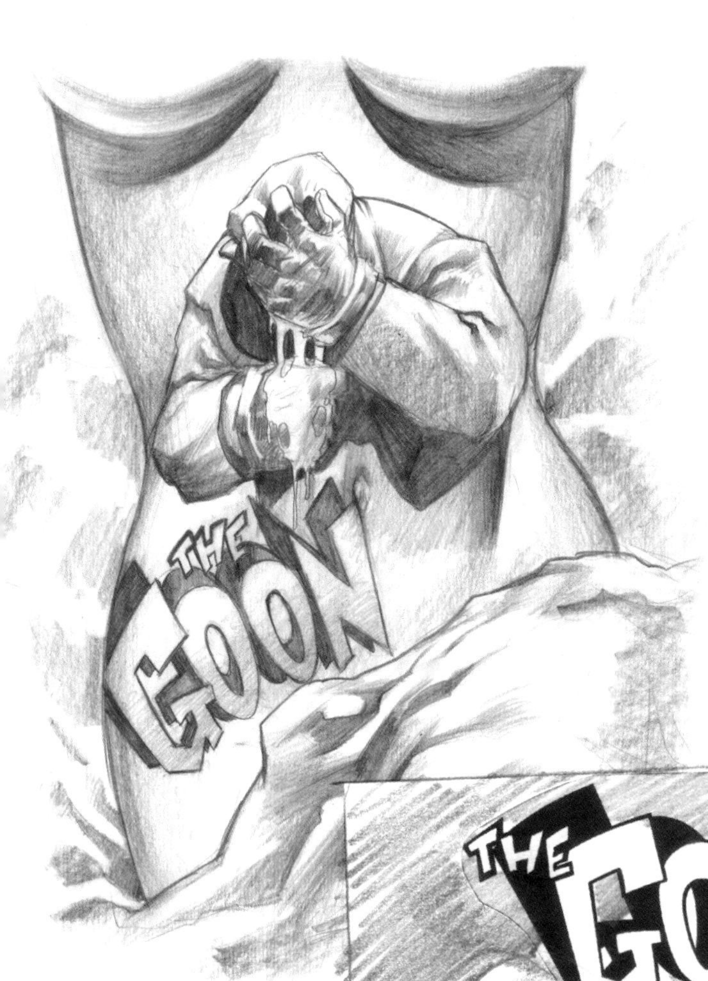
THE GOON

Early *Chinatown*
concepts.

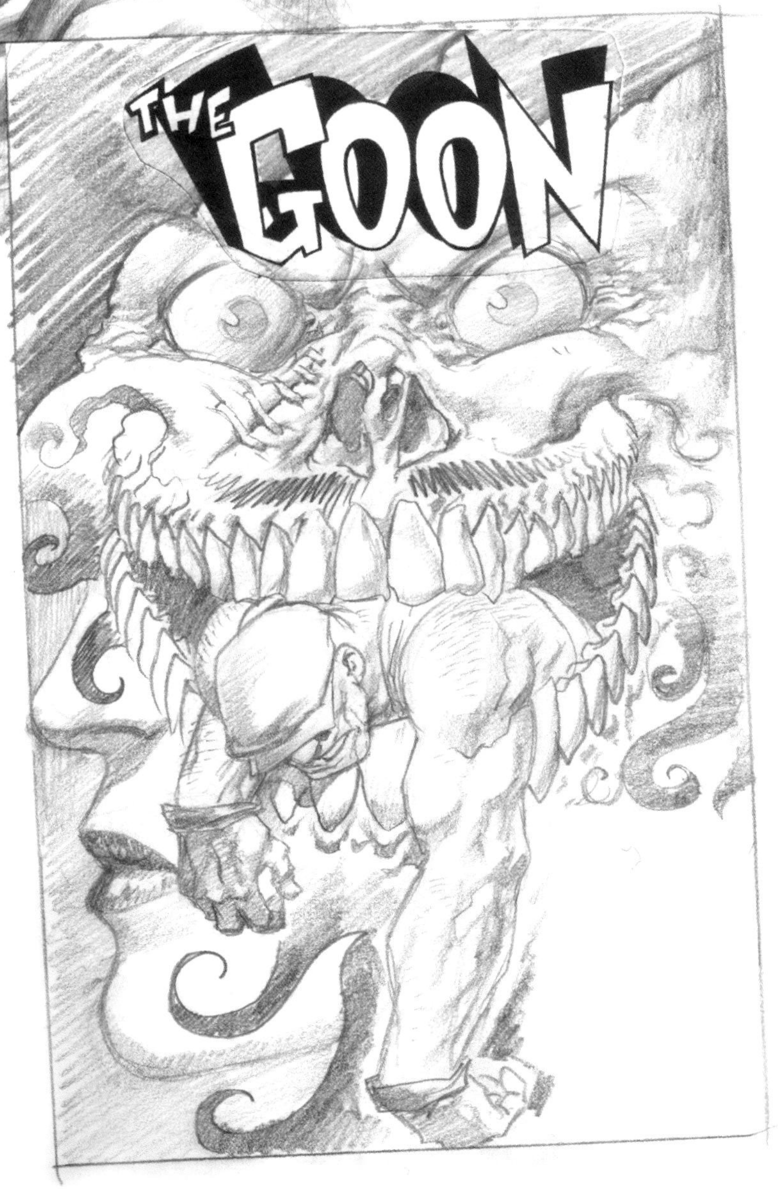
THE GOON

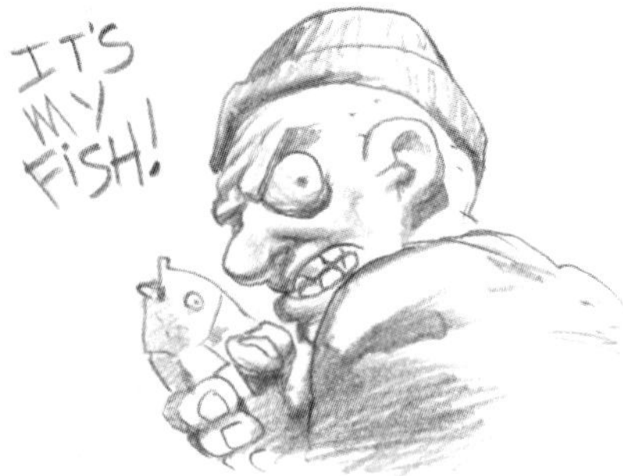
IT'S MY FISH!

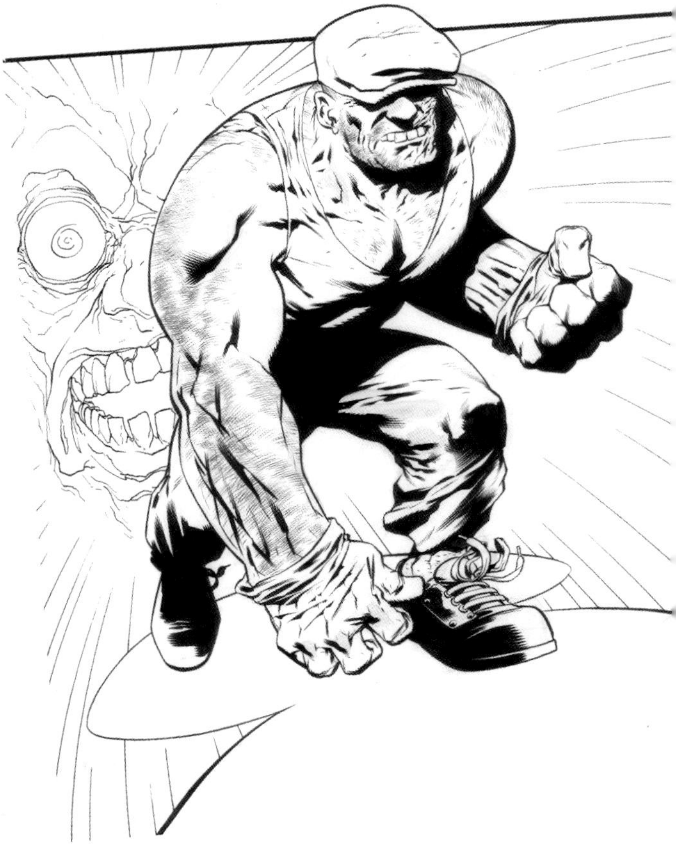

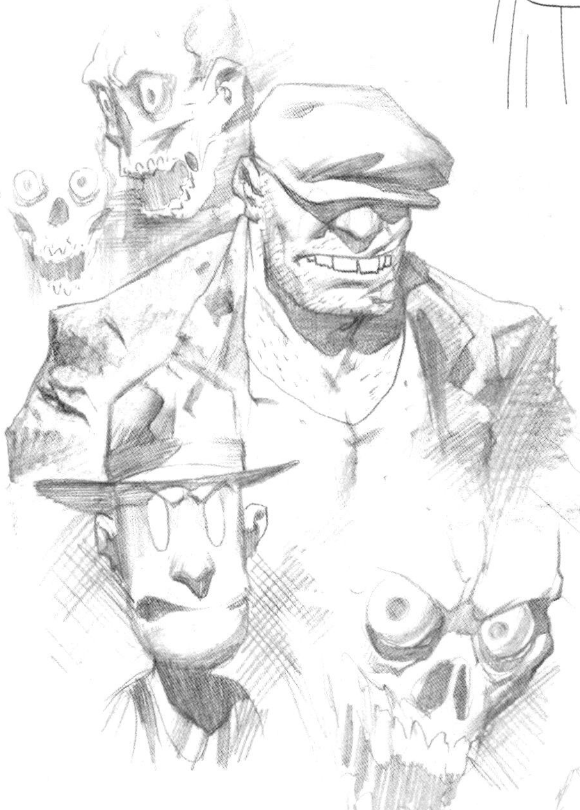

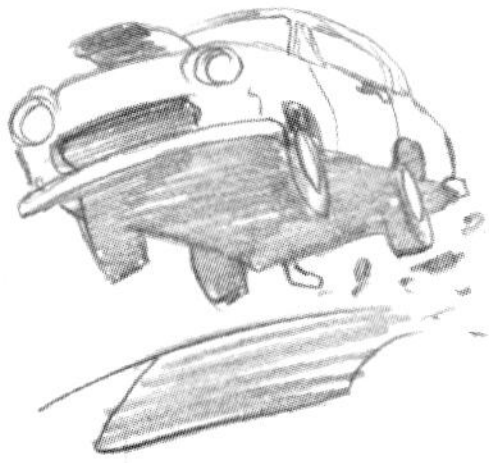

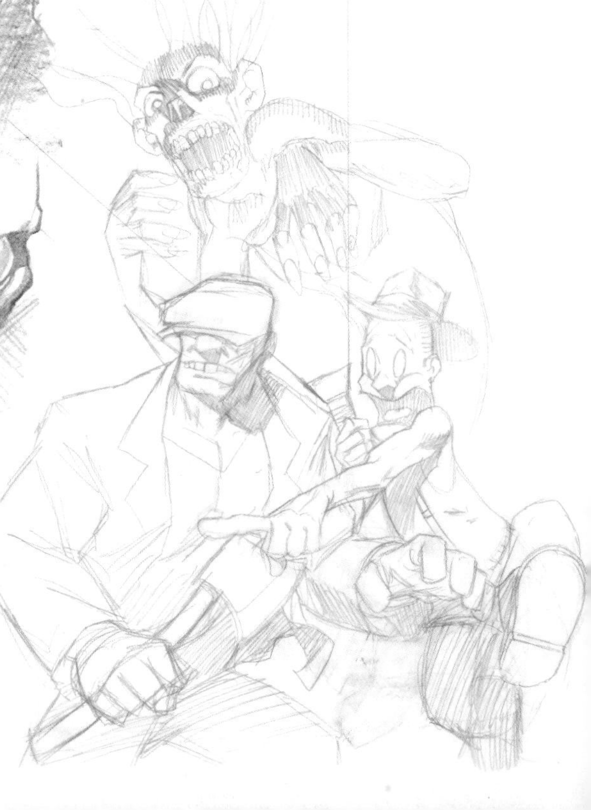

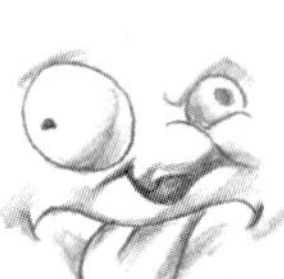

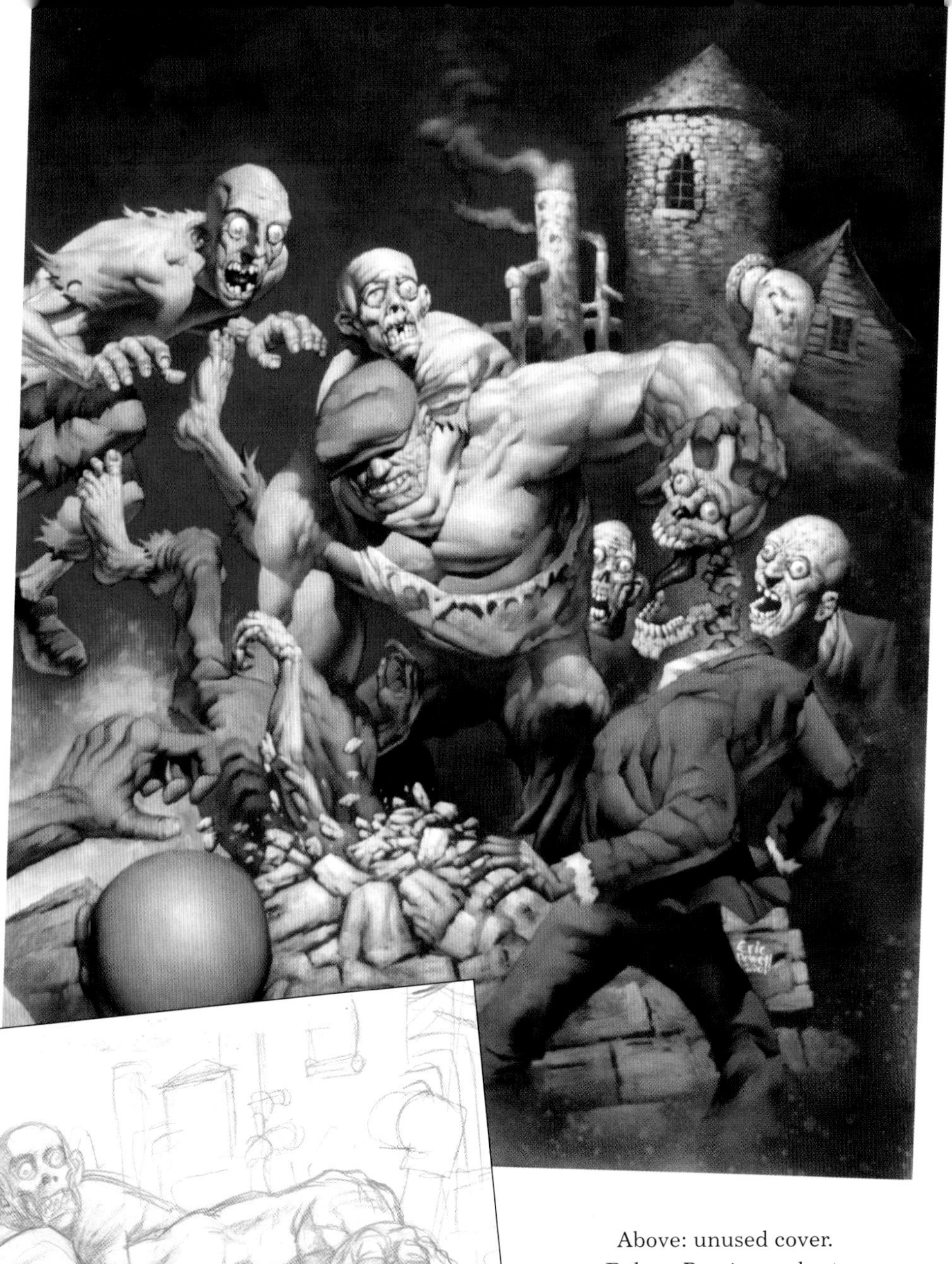

Above: unused cover.
Below: *Previews* ad art.

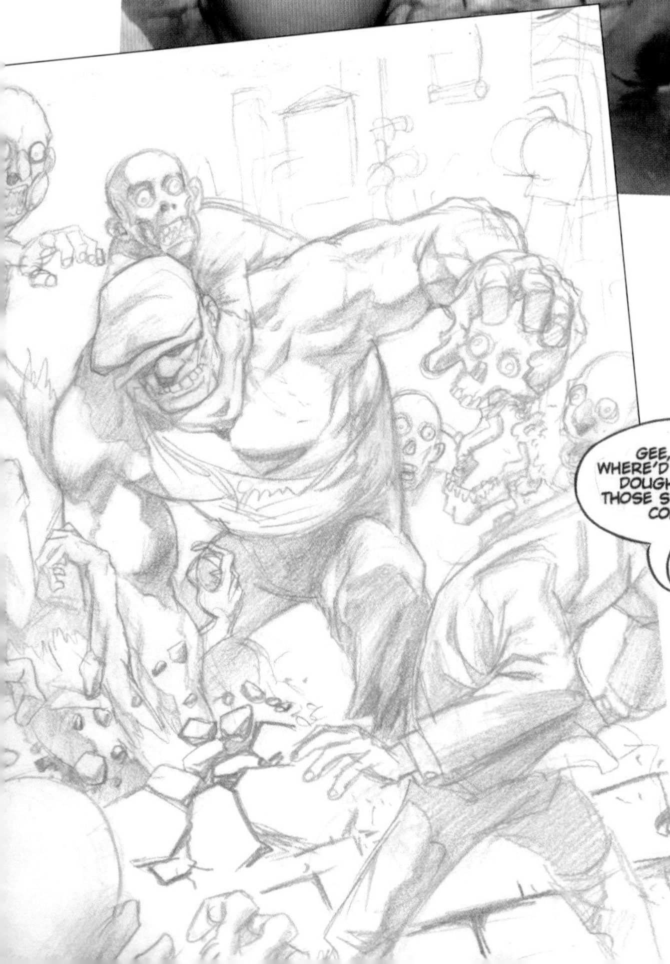

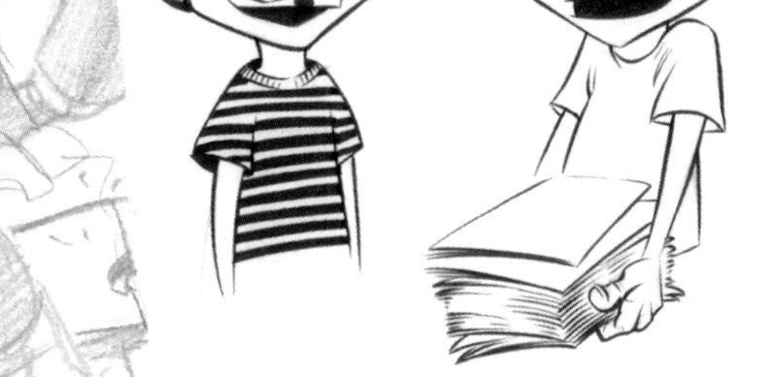
GEE, WALLY, WHERE'D YA GET THE DOUGH FOR ALL THOSE SWELL GOON COMICS?
I SOLD GRANPA'S HEART MEDICINE TO SOME TEEN AGE HOOLIGANS!